The Peacemakers

Selected Poems

WALDO WILLIAMS

translated by Tony Conran

First Impression—1997

ISBN 1 85902 440 0

This book is published with the support of the
Arts Council of Wales.

Printed in Wales at
Gomer Press, Llandysul, Ceredigion

ACKNOWLEDGEMENTS

Two translations ('Mewn Dau Gae'—'In Two Fields'—and 'Wedi'r Canrifoedd Mudan'—'After the Mute Centuries') first appeared in *The Penguin Book of Welsh Verse* (1967) and subsequently in *Welsh Verse* (Seren Books, 1986). Others have been printed in *Poetry Wales*, *The New Welsh Review*, *Translation* and *The Swansea Review*. Some of the Introduction, also, has been adapted from material first published in those journals.

I would like to thank Miss Dilys Williams, the poet's sister, for her graciousness in giving her blessing to the project before she had seen the result. It is impossible to thank all the friends who have helped me, but I would like to mention Eddie Lunt who came up to me at the Pontardawe Folk Festival, said he liked my Waldo versions in the Penguin, and demanded more; Nigel Jenkins who was kind enough to lend me a copy of his play about Waldo; the late Prof. Bedwyr Lewis Jones, Prof. Gwyn Thomas, Dafydd Glyn Jones and Gruffydd Aled Williams of the University College of North Wales, Bangor for being so constantly 'on call' when I needed them; and also James Nicholas, Gerallt Jones, the late Euros Bowen, and of course my own family. They have helped me in innumerable ways.

I have mentioned in the Introduction my gratitude to Prof. Joseph Clancy for allowing me to use one of his translations. I would like also to say how grateful I am to Prof. Dafydd Johnston of the University College of Swansea for rescuing me from my failure to translate Waldo's *awdl*, 'Tŷ Ddewi', with the offer of a prose version—see the appendix to this book.

My special thanks are due, however, to Dafydd Glyn Jones who has gone through my versions and through the introduction with great and painstaking care, correcting blunders and suggesting amendments. I owe him a great deal, not least for the insights into Waldo he has given me. Not that I've always agreed with him—and any mistakes that remain are certainly my responsibility not his—but it has been a great support for someone like myself to have him (as it were) underwriting my work.

CONTENTS

Introduction 9
A Note on the Translation 51

EARLY POEMS 1930-36
Mowth-organ · Mouth-organ 58
Yr Hen Allt · The Ancient Wood 60
Cofio · Remembering 62
Cwm Berllan · Cwm Berllan (Orchard Valley) 64

CERDDI'R PLANT—POETRY FOR CHILDREN (1936)
selected from the book by Waldo Williams and E. Llwyd Williams
Morgrugyn · Ant 68
Bore Nadolig · Christmas Morning 70
Chwarae · Playing 72

THE SECOND WORLD WAR— Poems published 1938-46
(with a few of uncertain date which belong here)
Y Tŵr a'r Graig · The Tower and the Rock [Opening sections] 76
Daw'r Wennol yn ôl i'w nyth · The Swallow will find her nest 78
Daffodil · Daffodil 80
Diwedd Bro · The End of a Countryside 82
O Bridd · O Soil of the Earth 84
Brawdoliaeth · Brotherhood 88
Y Tangnefeddwyr · The Peacemakers 90
Englynion y Rhyfel—Y Milwr · The Soldier 92
Ar Weun Cas' Mael · On Weun Cas' Mael 94
Linda · Linda 98
Dan y Dyfroedd Claear · Under the Gentle Waters 100
Y Plant Marw · The Dead Children 102
Cân Bom · Bomb Song 104

ACKNOWLEDGE—Poems published 1946-56 before the publication
of *Dail Pren*
Adnabod · Acknowledge 108
Preselau · Preseli 112
Caniad Ehedydd · Lark Song 114
Cwmwl Haf · A Summer Cloud 116
Cymru'n Un · Wales One 120

Cymru a Chymraeg · Welsh and Wales   122
Yr Heniaith · The Old Language   124
Y Geni · Nativity   126
Wedi'r Canrifoedd Mudan · After the Mute Centuries
    (the Catholic martyrs)   128
Pa Beth yw Dyn? · What is Man?   130
Mewn Dau Gae · In Two Fields   132
[Duw] o 'Paham yr wyf yn Grynwr' ·
    [God] from 'Why I am a Quaker'   136

LEAVES OF A TREE—Poems first published in *Dail Pren*, 1956
    (two poems, which belong here by publication, have been
    included in the Second World War section.]
Geneth Ifanc · A Young Girl   140
Oherwydd ein Dyfod · Because of our coming   142
Angharad · Angharad   144
Gyfaill, mi'th Gofiaf · I remember a friend   146
Tri Bardd o Sais a Lloegr · Three English Poets and England 148
Eirlysiau · Snowdrops   152
Heb Deitl · Untitled   154
Yr Eiliad · The Moment   156
Yn Nyddiau'r Cesar · In the Days of Caesar   158
Eneidfawr · Great-Soul   160
Y Ci Coch · The Red Dog   162
Medi · Harvest   164

LATER POEMS 1960-70
Llwyd · Llwyd   168
Cân imi, wynt · Sing to me, Wind   172
Gwenallt · Gwenallt   174
Y Dderwen Gam · The Crooked Oak   176
Llandysilio-yn-Nyfed · Llandysilio-yn-Nyfed   178

APPENDIX
Tŷ Ddewi · St David's (1936, revised 1956)   182
    (translation by Dafydd Johnston of the *awdl* 'Tŷ Ddewi'

NOTES TO THE POEMS   208

NOTES TO THE APPENDIX   212

INTRODUCTION

'Have you read this?' Amy said. '"Why I Refuse To Pay My Income Tax."'

It was an article in a Welsh weekly magazine I subscribed to that Amy did not often read—or claimed not to . . .

'Do you know this man?' she said. 'He sounds very much like one of your lot.'

A schoolteacher called Davies had resigned his job to prevent the government, in the shape of the local authority, deducting income tax from his salary and using it to send national servicemen to Korea. Is it from such simplistic gestures that prophets are born? 'One of your lot' means almost anyone holding what she has now come to regard as extremist views, about war, about the language, about the land and the community, about self-government or about anything that might inconvenience a Labour Party and government in which she had invested her unflagging hopes of advancement. She nibbled at her lower lip as she devoured the article and I saw her party allegiance shadow the paper like the hat on her head.

'Well,' she said. 'It appears that Mr Davies has vowed to go to prison before he will allow any pennies he earns to be used to arm young conscripts and send them to Korea.'

She was smiling as she said it. She found Davies's stand outlandish and eccentric in the extreme. She didn't find it in any way related to her own behaviour when she was young and glowing with ideals. She had been beautiful in her defiance. I tried to remember what Davies looked like. I had met him at an Eisteddfod. A small tubby man in tweeds full of jokes as I recalled; too many for my taste. He and his cronies eddied around the eisteddfod field held together by what I took to be a mucilage of mutual admiration, feeding off their own wit and hoping to collide at any moment with groups of kindred spirits.

'He has great faith in the peoples of the earth getting to know each other,' Amy said. 'The brotherhood of man and so on. How does a North Korean get to know a South Korean except with a bullet?'

She was roused by the article in spite of herself. It was an opportunity, it seemed to me; an opening . . .

Emyr Humphreys: *Bonds of Attachment*, pp. 309-310.

John Cilydd More's response to this article occasions the final break-up of his marriage with Amy Parry in the last of Emyr Humphreys' sequence of novels that began with *National Winner*. It leads to his suicide. The passage I have quoted is fictionalised, but anyone who knows the cultural history of Wales will recognise in the intransigent schoolmaster the poet and pacifist Waldo Williams.[1] It is largely a hostile portrait. Davies is seen through the eyes of Cilydd, a successful eisteddfod-winner in the past but now largely bitter and out-of-touch; and of Amy, who has become part of the Labour Party establishment. Cilydd remembers him as a too-persistent humourist, a member of an eisteddfod sub-culture, a group bound together by wit and mutual admiration, not able to reach the top but perpetually looking for the reassurance of new recruits. Amy sees him only in terms of his political stand which she finds 'outlandish and eccentric in the extreme.'

Nevertheless, both find themselves deeply challenged by this tubby and vaguely pathetic pacifist's article. Amy is roused by it in spite of herself. Cilydd sees it as an opportunity, an opening—that is, in the first instance, an opportunity to communicate with Amy again; but ultimately as an opening for frustrated idealism into significant social activity. Cilydd fails to make the right response, thinking only of the need to protect Davies from the consequences of his action; in doing so, he precipitates the family's collapse and his own suicide.

Davies's position is sarcastically summarised by Amy as a 'great faith in the peoples of the earth getting to know each other. The brotherhood of man and so on.' As we shall see, each of these terms, ('faith', 'peoples of the earth,' 'getting to know each other'—*adnabod* in Welsh—and 'the brotherhood of man') was in fact crucial to Waldo's poetry and to his life. Davies in *Bonds of Attachment* may be a hostile portrait of Waldo, but as far as it goes it is not altogether unfair. There is a side of Waldo Williams which corresponds to the tubby humourist seeking consolation for his failure in the mutual admiration and 'mucilage' of an in-group feeding off its own wit. A great deal of Welsh cultural life—certainly in the nineteen-fifties—might appear to the outsider (and not only to the outsider) as like that: a less advanced state of the disease which Raymond Williams identifies in O'Casey's Dublin, where brilliant talk becomes a substitute for emotions which are too painful to confront. And certainly, the idealism and sense of brotherhood that Waldo had in such fullness could, in its very humility, appear outlandish and eccentric in the extreme.

Waldo's challenge to Welsh mores is successfully registered in the novel; but what the fiction leaves out (for its own good reasons) is that Waldo was a great poet, not simply a near-miss at the eisteddfod; and that he became one of the best-loved people in Welsh Wales. And, obviously, it cannot see with Waldo's eyes, or express the quality of his inner life, its rootedness and joy, and its profound suffering.

Waldo Williams was born in 1904 at Haverfordwest in Pembrokeshire. His father was a primary-school teacher who came from the Pembrokeshire countryside, whose first language was Welsh; but his mother Angharad, though her family came from what is now Denbighshire, was born in Shropshire and brought up English-speaking, so that English was Waldo's mother tongue. He did not speak Welsh until he was seven, when he learnt it in the playground of the school at Mynachlog-ddu where his father was then headmaster. English remained an important part of his life. He graduated in English at Aberystwyth. He was profoundly influenced by English poetry. At least twice in his life, once after the outbreak of the 1939-45 war when he went on holiday to the Quantock Hills in Somerset, and then, even more dramatically, for six years after the sudden death of his wife Linda, he sought refuge in rural, poetic England from emotional trauma in Wales.[2] The Quantocks were where Wordsworth recovered from the French Revolution and the alienation he felt when England declared war on France; and where he and Coleridge wrote *Lyrical Ballads*, usually taken to be the beginning of the Romantic movement. Waldo's later six-year stay was also, as he tells us in 'Tri Bardd o Sais a Lloegr' ('Three English Poets and England'), a kind of pilgrimage round districts associated with Hardy, Keats and Cowper, in whose example he found comfort and strength.

Waldo's early poetry was that of a somewhat uneasy Georgian. He kept a few lyrics from this period in his only published collection *Dail Pren* (Leaves of a Tree) where they are scattered among later and much more rugged work; pieces like 'Mowth-organ' or 'Cwm Berllan' seem almost like holiday snaps, simple in feeling and undemanding in texture. Two poems from this period, however, while they retain this simplicity, also look forward to the weight and subject-matter of his later poetry. 'Yr Hen Allt' ('The Old Wood') reflects on the hopeful silly-sooth of recovery in Wales after the 1914-18 war; and 'Cofio' ('Remembering')—probably still his most popular poem—seeks to hold and acknowledge (*adnabod*) the 'unremembered things of humankind', 'primitive' people and their languages, their exploits, their experience of children. It is a finer poem than one is at first inclined to credit; but to me at any rate its form (quatrains with feminine endings reminiscent of Emily Brontë) is all the time tipping the balance towards nostalgia rather than the active imagination and 'acknowledgement' that the theme demands.

As with so many Georgian poets in both English and Welsh, one registers an uncertainty of direction in this early work and a spillage of the imagination into other modes—in this case, light verse and parody, and writing for children. I have translated very little of this: parody is almost impossible to translate, because it relies on a moment by moment recognition of the original, and light verse, often topical, often relying on word-play or the neatness of rhymes that are unavailable in a different language, very quickly seems to lose its savour. The writing for children is, I think, more central to our awareness of Waldo as a great poet, despite its slightness, and I have tried to represent his work here by some examples—both from *Cerddi'r Plant* (*Poems for Children*) which he published in collaboration with E. Llwyd Williams, and the little *cywydd* 'Y Ci Coch' ('The Red Dog') from *Dail Pren*.

But there was always more to Waldo than a minor Georgian. Two things levered him out of that cul-de-sac. One was the strict-metre tradition of Welsh poetry: he competed—albeit unsuccessfully—for the Chair in the National Eisteddfod at Fishguard in 1936 with an *awdl* (long ode in the strict metres) on 'Tŷ Ddewi', that is, St David's, the cathedral in Pembrokeshire.[3] It is in three sections. The first, 'Bore' ('Morning'), is about the coming of Christianity to Wales: Dewi Sant (St David) meets an old fisherman who rejects the new faith because of his love for the old Celtic religion. Dewi tells him that the 'old beauty of Brân the Blessed' and the ancient gods will not be lost: the imagination itself is fulfilled in Christ.

The second part, 'Canol Dydd' ('Mid Day'), concerns the cathedral in the middle ages, when it became a centre of pilgrimage. A stonemason working there longs for the old solitude of Dewi's cell instead of the bustle of pilgrims that now frequent it—a solitude that is not incompatible with the New Jerusalem of all witnesses to Christ, where time and oppression will not penetrate.

The third part, 'Hwyr' ('Evening'), recounts a sort of mystical experience Waldo had had on Carn Llidi, a hill near St Davids. Time seemed to be conquered, and he looked beyond all the oppression and violence that had scarred the world, into its pristine reality.

Waldo wrote the poem hastily (James Nicholas talks of it being the concentrated work of two weekends[4]) and he did not revise it until 1956—in fact, the text in *Dail Pren* was considerably rewritten. Nevertheless, it opened up huge possibilities for his poetry, dealing as it does with what for him were central issues: the coming of Christianity and its relation to the poetic imagination; the values of solitude and their relation to community; and the timeless moment and its relationship to time. More than that, it localised the apprehension of the eternal in a topography that he had known and loved all his life, his own *bro* or native district, the coasts and hills of Pembrokeshire. It set the pattern of his work as a local poet—not just as Wordsworth or Hardy are local poets in English, though it included that; but also as a writer who served his own community and celebrated its past and present as part of it himself. But of course Dewi in the poem is much more than a Pembrokeshire worthy: he is the patron saint of Wales, apostle of the Universal Church, peacemaker and visionary. Already, perhaps, he represents that alternative society of peace that Waldo was to find struggling into existence, as it were, in Welsh community-life, and which he set against the war-mongering sovereignty of the state.

The strict metres tightened and jarred against the Georgian easiness of his early work. They allowed him fellowship with his hero, T. Gwynn Jones, the great poet of the early part of the twentieth century who had made poetry speak for the civilization of Wales as no one had done since the middle ages. Like Gwynn Jones, Waldo was obsessed by a vision: its realization in both the community and in the individual imagination was what his poetry was about. For both poets, *cynghanedd*—the verbal soundplay of strict-metre poetry—was a talisman and a tool that had to do with embodying vision.

For T. Gwynn Jones, the quest was tragic. The civilization was doomed, the imagination that conceived it committed suicide rather than submit to the vulgarity of what succeeded. In his later poetry he abandoned *cynghanedd* as he accepted his vision's defeat. But for Waldo Williams, the eternal still held. He is not a tragic writer, because ultimately, for him, history does not change anything. Peace and war, love and hatred, reality and illusion—they do not change.

13

Peacemakers are blessed, they inherit the earth. The just man justices, as Hopkins says, whether in the stone age or twentieth-century Haverfordwest. Which is not to deny the suffering—indeed, the suffering is what moral struggle is about:

> The tree of the worlds is lofty
> But in September now
> The great ripe sun is bending
> The branches of it low.
>
> So too beneath its burden
> A more ancient tree is fraught,
> Inclining through the stillness
> Down towards man's heart.
>
> And between earth's seasons
> Puts on a different face.
> Amid the perpetual warfare
> Of Michael, there is peace.

That poem was written much later, of course, when Waldo could actually use the hated word 'rhyfel'—war—for the struggles of the angelic host.

The strict metres gave him a framework, almost a platform, which he could use to steady himself and develop his own vision. It is noteworthy how much of his poetry in the late thirties uses *cynghanedd* to put forward the values of peace; at the end of his life, after his major poetry was written and published, he turned again to the strict metres to become a sort of apotheosis of the *bardd gwlad*, community poet or poet of a locality, writing to his neighbours and friends *cywyddau* that joyously sing of the 'husbandry of the neighbourhood of God'—'hwsmonaeth cymdogaeth Duw' as he puts in his great elegy for Llwyd.

The other purchase that levered him out of Georgianism was of course the approaching war with Germany. His second long poem of the period, 'Y Tŵr a'r Graig' ('The Tower and the Rock') was a sequence of *cywyddau* (singular *cywydd*, a strict-metre poem in couplets) occasioned by a proposal in the House of Lords to introduce military conscription. Again he takes the topography of Dyfed as a paradigm: the tower, representing militarism and the sovereignty it gives rise to, is Roch Castle:

14

Left from a war long ago,
Violence sleeps in its shadow,
Up into air, a stronghold
Black into deep sky is bold.
To the seawind, sharp outline,
Beetle-browed above the brine,
Without hawks of war, still stands
On the civilized headland.
Despite all revolution
Stiff is that wide-watching one.
But where are the sharp arrows
From the sinews of yew bows?
Where's the cold thin spear? the arms?
The kin of conqueror William?
Where are the hosts of battle?
The warriors? and the grim earl?

It is a deserted ruin now, but the power that put it there still stalks the land, taking away the people's freedom and putting poverty where there was wealth.

The rock on the other hand (Plumstead Rock as well as Roch Castle were both visible from his childhood home in Llandysilio) stands both for a refuge and for what might be called the Romantic Covenant, a sign that, as Wordsworth in 'Tintern Abbey' put it, Nature never did betray the heart that loved her; and more than that, a sign that God loves his people, with a care that the Tower exists to deny:

Over there's a bare summit,
An old rock, a boulder on it
By the pale lip of the sea,
A rough stone for a boundary—
Under grey clouds a great word
To a prophet discovered.
Those who acknowledge it, the stone
Loves like a fellow dalesman
Humble and poor, yet higher
In its vigilance and care
Raising up above the rim
Of the world, our lives' burden.
That word spoken from the cairn
Outlasts the age of iron.

15

But despite his hope and idealism, war when it came devastated him:

> 'My great bow Gandiva', says Arjuna in the Bhagavad-Gita, 'falls from my hands, and the skin of my flesh is burning; I am no longer able to stand because my mind is whirling and wandering.'

That moment of horror before the nightmare of fratricide is echoed in Waldo Williams's poems from the early forties. 'O Bridd,' for instance, 'O soil of the earth,' is a wildly expressionistic piece where he sees the very soil we live on as evil and corrupt—

> Your red flowers are pox,
> Your yellow flowers pus.
> I'll not move. I've nowhere to go.
> Your fever has moved to my blood.
> I've seen the filthy maw
> Open and say, 'Ho, brother'—
> In the blood pit, my brother's
> Squeal sucked through his nape,
> Legs and no feet, my brother . . .
>
> She pushes us behind, our mother.
> She grimaces through the window.
> Shouts, 'Ho, people, providence!'
> She cackles over destruction.

The poem ends with a vision of God waiting in the Antarctic wastes: the only real value is in the absence of soil, the negation of life. Arjuna falls into despair because he is required to fight and kill the members of his actual family; but of course Waldo's despair is more universal because he believes *all* men are his brothers. 'O Bridd' marks a fundamentally immature position where it is impossible to stay sane for very long. Waldo was rescued from it by his relationship with his wife Linda before her early death, and by his own faith in the goodness of things struggling to be good; but he kept 'O Bridd' in his collection, presumably as a touchstone of the nightmare he and the world had suffered at that time.

It may seem strange to call Waldo Williams a great war-poet—but what else is he?— though he never fought in battle, and never gave countenance to the idea that war was ever necessary. When, later on (as we've seen) he realised that the taxes he paid were going towards the war in Korea he resigned from his job where taxes were deducted P.A.Y.E., and went to prison rather than pay them. His whole work is a protest against violence: of all the possible attitudes to armed conflict that poets can take—Rupert Brooke, Edward Thomas, Wilfred Owen, David Jones, Alun Lewis, Sorley MacLean—his is the most extreme in its opposition. Against war he put peace, against the warrior he put the saint, against the sovereignty of the nation he put community and the kinship of all mankind.

Waldo Williams' poetry is astonishingly varied, in form and intention; but at its heart his inspiration is all of a piece. To see this, and to appreciate how deeply his pacifism penetrated his work, I want to look neither at his large-scale masterpieces such as 'Y Tŵr a'r Graig' ('The Tower and the Rock') or 'Mewn Dau Gae' ('In Two Fields') nor at his more obviously anti-war poems, but at his very last sonnet of all, 'Llandysilio-yn-Nyfed,' about a village in Welsh-speaking Pembrokeshire where he spent much of his boyhood. The name means 'St Tysilio-in-Dyfed.' Here is the poem:

LLANDYSILIO-YN-NYFED

I am often amazed. What light came from beyond
   That to his elect ones Christ could reveal
When life for us was brutal, full of wrong,
   Made great by neither purpose nor ideal?
I remember how we'd all go to the door
   When the church bell rang for a better year—
Maldwyn's gentleness on Dyfed once more
   As the imagination far and near
Travelled deep night. We'd see small companies,
   Without exploit of cities, yoke the world one
And among them, salvation clear, we'd see
   In the white flame rejoicing for God's son
Tysilio, who rather than draw his sword
Chose exile here, ceased to be Meifod's lord.

It seems at first sight a fairly innocuous 'local' poem about the patron saint of a village church. Of course, it refers back to the Age of the Saints—the sixth century or thereabouts when Wales became a Christian country. It was a time constantly in Waldo's mind, and a matrix of his own crusade against 'sovereignty' and war, because

17

when monks like Gildas failed to persuade the warlords to mend their ways, they turned aside and founded instead their own alternative society devoted to peace. Tysilio was a lord of Powys in the sixth century who chose the monastic life. He lived in Meifod in Maldwyn—the old Montgomeryshire, proverbial for its gentleness—but had to escape because some of his family tried to make him a prince.

That, then, is the Saint—Tysilio in an age of cruelty and greed given the light of Christ 'from beyond,' and joining in small companies to 'yoke the world one' into peace. Christ in Waldo Williams is chiefly the peacemaker of the Beatitudes, the teacher who spoke in the parables. Whether the poet believed that Christ saved him from his own personal sinfulness and damnation, and chose him to go to heaven—whether he was an orthodox Christian at all—is very doubtful. He certainly had mystical intimations of the coming of God's kingdom; but his most famous expression of these (in 'Mewn Dau Gae'—'In Two Fields') is rooted in ordinary people working together in the fields, not in any Christian Second Coming. Jesus, Tysilio, Mahatma Gandhi—people who are prepared to suffer in this world for the cause of brotherhood and peace—are those who have the light of Christ revealed to them. As he says in his poem about the raids on Swansea, thinking of his parents,

> In Christ's light is freedom had
> For any man that would be free.
> Blest, the day dawns that will hear them,
> Peacemakers, children of God.
>
> ('The Peacemakers')

But in fact the sonnet is not primarily about Tysilio. It is called 'Llandysilio-yn-Nyfed,' the parish, the village community gathered round Tysilio's church; and about Waldo himself as a boy as part of that community. It remembers the experience of waiting outside for the New Year, of the bells ringing and the family going indoors filled with wonder. Such ritual interruptions of the everyday are designed to release the imagination to make contact with what is important—in this case, the Light that manifested Christ to Tysilio. On a purely empirical level, that is what the poem is about. It is a picture of a community in action, at one of its moments of remembrance and hope, taking sustenance from the past to give to the future. It is this 'brotherhood,' that Waldo always opposes to 'sovereignty' and temporal power. Like the early monks round Tysilio, it is a community 'without exploit of cities,' a small company that yet 'yokes the world one.'

But even that is not what the sonnet is really about. Its first sentence is not about the past, neither Tysilio's exile nor Waldo's own boyhood. It begins with the present: 'Mynych rwy'n syn'- 'Often I'm amazed.' What should give us a jolt is the full stop. One is tempted to read it as simply, 'I am often amazed by the way light came from beyond to illumine Christ to Tysilio and his chosen ones,' and so on, making it just the pious amazement of a Church historian. But it isn't that. 'Often I am amazed.' As one reads the poem, one suddenly sees that there are three times involved, each with its own future implied. First (in inverse order of appearance) there is the time of Tysilio's choice of exile rather than the power of the sword, when the small companies of monks yoked the world one and salvation was like a clear flame. Secondly there is the poet's own boyhood, on New Year's eve, when the bells of the church rang in hope for a better year. And thirdly, there is now, the poet being amazed.

Read in this way, the lines about the light coming to reveal Christ to the elect ones when *our* life (*ein* byw—my italics) was greedy and cruel, without any great purpose or ideal—these lines need not simply refer to the collapse of values after the fall of Rome. After all, the Dark Ages were not the only time where life has been cruel, greedy and lacking in ideals. Like all Waldo's mature work his last poem refers ultimately to the struggle against Sovereignty and war-making now and in his own lifetime. The amazingness of the Light making clear the ways of Peace and the rescue of community and brotherhood in the teeth of war—that's what he wonders at, 'mynych,' often—in fact, one could almost say, always. 'Llandysilio-yn-Nyfed' is as much a war-poem, in its own way, as 'Dan y Dyfroedd Claear' ('Under the Gentle Waters)' after one of the great battles of the Pacific, or 'The Peacemakers'—

> Rose-red sky above the snow
>   Where bombed Swansea is alight,
> Full of my father and mother I go,
>   I walk home in the night.

They are blest beyond hearing,
Peacemakers, children of God . . .

What is their estate tonight,
    Tonight, with the world ablaze?
Truth is with my father yet,
    Mother with forgiveness stays.
The age will be blest that hears them,
Peacemakers, children of God.

        *   *   *

Welsh poetry has tended to be a very masculine affair. The great poets of its twentieth-century renaissance—T. Gwynn Jones, Williams Parry, Saunders Lewis and Gwenallt—have all been essentially men talking to men. The eisteddfod is a male world: not many Welsh poets would describe their art even as Dafydd ap Gwilym does, as—

> Cerdd a genir ymhob gwledd
> I ddiddanu rhianedd

('a poem is sung at every feast to entertain young girls') or to put such entertainment on a par with 'prayer in the church to gain the land of Paradise.' But even Dafydd is rarely prepared to take feminine viewpoints seriously, as an expression of our common humanity.

So it is with politics: the great politician is the leader of the pack, the male hunting group. Mabon, Lloyd George, Nye Bevan are always thought of as orators—almost like Roman generals—urging their forces into action. The one apparent exception is 'Rebecca' and her 'daughters' in the nineteenth century riots against toll-gates—very largely in the same area as Waldo came from, incidentally. The meetings of Rebecca were clandestine, anonymous and nocturnal, whereas political meetings are usually open, the leaders well-known, and often take place under the wide light of day. Rebecca's feminine disguise was partly an inversion of this norm, therefore, an expression of another side of the brain being in control. To go in drag to a destruction of private property has its saturnalian aspects. But it also conjured deep feelings, as the elaborately acted-out rituals of Rebecca 'the old Mother' before the toll-gates show. The rioters spoke in the name of domestic economy, the woman's private world, affronted and threatened by commercial greed. Nor should we discount the repudiation of armed conflict in the woman's clothing. Neither Rebecca nor any of her successors in the 'politics of the night' has ever gone out with the intention of endangering life. They have never been serious para-military movements like the I.R.A. or the French Resistance.

Rebecca's daughters were in drag; but they were still the equivalent, even with the qualifications that that implied, of a male hunting pack. The nocturnal and secret expedition to destroy property in the name of a higher law has represented an alternative way of politics in Wales ever since. The history of Welsh nationalism veers from day to night and back again, many times. Except in the very early period when it was dominated by Saunders Lewis, day-time politics, in the shape of political party, rally and summer school, has nearly always tried to disown the politics of the night. Again, the contrast with Ireland is striking. There has never been a real equivalent to Gerry Adams's Sinn Fein, a 'political wing' of the arsonists of second homes. To an extent, though, in non-violent contexts the Welsh Language Society has played both roles.

Welsh politics and Welsh poetry came together most strikingly in the figure of Saunders Lewis, the founder of Plaid Cymru, literally the Party of Wales. And we must note how Zealot-like and male his whole approach was. If you are oppressed by other people's politics, then the thing to do is to start a politics of your own. You too can marshal your troops, you too can form a clandestine resistance. You can go out with your hunting group and burn down the enemy's bombing school. The fact that Saunders was not merely a Rebecca in bard's clothing but also a daylight politician meant that his expedition had to be a bit incompetent and amateur, and also that the would-be guerrillas had to give themselves up at the nearest police station. Saunders Lewis's attempt to reconcile the two politics of day and night was like a bungled martyrdom, too costly in human terms to have successors in modern Wales.

But both politics were pretty much male affairs, like the poetry. With Waldo Williams, on the other hand, as with Christ, we find the presence of women at the very core of his experience and thought. His mother, his sisters and his wife are quite crucially involved both in his greatness as a poet, and in the political reality he represents. Nor is this simply a matter of his own need for feminine comfort and

21

reassurance, though that is certainly present. His whole philosophy is that of a carer: his greatest moral imperative is 'adnabod'— acknowledging, recognising others, loving them as we love and know ourselves.

Both his own childhood and the children he saw suffer are therefore, as they were to Christ, paradigms of the Kingdom of God. It was as a child that he realised the community of men working in the fields together, the experience which lies behind the mystical waiting for the Exiled King of 'Mewn Dau Gae', or the need to protect the deep springs of 'Preseli'. There are photographs of Waldo among the children he taught: they can be compared with those of Idris Davies, also a primary-school teacher. Whereas Idris Davies is always seen posed for a school photo, with the children sitting in rows and the teachers at the ends looking smug and uncomfortable, Waldo has been caught in a relaxed way shepherding the children towards the camera, almost one of themselves. Of course to a certain extent, it's the luck of the draw: the photographer happened to catch him like that. All the same, it seems right. Children respond to the child in the teacher, as much as they do to the grown-up with designs on them as potential achievers.

The prophet of 'adnabod' is confident in his spiritual message:

> I believe Divine Sympathy to be the full self realisation of the Imagination that brought forth the world . . . It tells us that it would be wrong and therefore futile, to seek even justice, even justice for others, through the slaughter and bereavement and mutilation and misery of multitudes of men, women and children. It tells us that oppression is not shortly to be eliminated from the world . . .[5]

But as we've seen in 'O Bridd' ('O Soil of the Earth') he experienced also moments, hours, months when nothing made sense and his whole being was frozen in panic and horror. This alternation of 'living in eternity's sunrise' (as Blake might say) with 'fallings from us, vanishings' and extreme existential despair seems to have haunted him all his life. One of his greatest poems 'Cwmwl Haf' ('A Summer Cloud') registers such a moment of panic in his childhood.

It is a strange piece, particularly when one first reads it. You can hear the gears clanking as it moves from one thing to another, and it ends with grammar itself buckling under the torrential expression of recollected feelings. It is one of his very few poems where (as with the childhood passages in Wordsworth's *Prelude*) the whole point seems to be the description of personal experience.

It opens with a roll-call of the names people give their houses—'Durham,' 'Devonia,' 'Allendale': the shock of the English names leads one to think Waldo is lamenting how English incomers are taking over the Welsh countryside. His point is much more human than that, however. (In fact, the poem was written in England!) All these names, he says, are really the same name,

> Name of the old place and the slow source of time
> In the cave that is brighter than air,
> The house that is out in all weathers.

The contrasts inherent in our homes, womb-like caves and yet (like shepherds) out in all weathers, have something of Bethlehem in them. They establish a polarity of inside and outside that is typical of Waldo in both his poetry and his politics: for the kind of political life he initiated was neither that of day nor of night, but of home, the slow source of time that is yet 'out in all weathers.'

There follows an idealised picture of his own childhood in the Pembrokeshire countryside, an idyll not untouched with humour as when the children think 'the great travelling stallion' is too big for his boots ('dangos ei bedolau'). The wonderful portrait of the cow seems straight out of ancient Mesopotamian or Egyptian religion:

> . . . see, up from the river
> A mildness, a milch dignity, like night
> Bending the rushes with her udders
> And on her horns carrying the sky.

And in this half mythical world of childhood, the grown-ups were like lords of language, greater than history-book kings and queens.

> In every weather, security was the weather.
> Lovingkindness was the house.

Into this idyll comes 'a spectre of a huge giant' without warning, suddenly all round him,

> A dank and grey stillness,
> The one that is waiting for us—

23

like death itself. Inside and outside in this nightmare are horribly confused. 'The world is too huge to exist,' he says. 'There is no there' ('Nid oes acw'). There is nothing but himself—'Dim ond fi yw yma'—the ungrammatical phrase has been compared to Rimbaud's 'Je est un autre'—something like 'Only I is here,' without father or mother, brother or sister, with the beginning and the end closing round him. (Presumably the poem was too early for Waldo to have heard of the cosmologists' Black Hole, but it does express a remarkable psychological equivalent to the closing of the 'event horizon' that black holes imply.)

Waldo panics, and tries to reach home—if there is home. It's like a seizure, almost what one imagines an epileptic must feel. He crosses the stream, touches the gatepost in an agony of doubt, and *before* he quite reaches the back door, a new creation has happened: he hears in the sound of his mother's clogs on the kitchen floor a new earth and a new heaven being built.

Is this a real new beginning, or just the reassertion of the power of the Welsh mam to give comfort and order? Feminists should I think steer carefully here, because although it is the mother's presence that validates the reality of inside and outside again, that reality was already coming into focus. He feels the gatepost, the mass of it. It is *there*.

At all events, this pattern was certainly reasserted at least twice in his adult life: once, as we've seen, after the outbreak of war, when he wrote 'O Bridd' and was restored to spiritual health by Linda taking him for a holiday in the Quantocks; and then, even more significantly, after Linda died and he escaped to England from the dereliction he felt in Wales. The poem that he eventually wrote about these events is 'Tri Bardd o Sais a Lloegr,' 'Three English Poets and England.'[6]

Ostensibly it is about what the title says it is, three English poets— Hardy, Keats and Cowper—and England, or at least being with his wife in the English countryside and giving thanks for that experience. Waldo and Linda were in England together only once, as far as I know, in the Quantock hills, Somerset, probably in Spring 1940. Anna Wyn Jones quotes a letter from him[7] where he talks about his feeling that the world was poisoned, hopelessly evil, after the outbreak of the Second World War. He says,

Dyna'r pryd y newidiais nôl, lawr yn Alfoxden a Nether Stowey. Aeth Linda a minnau yno yn y gwanwyn, y mannau lle sgrifennodd Wordsworth a Coleridge y Lyrical Ballads.

It was then I was restored, down in Alfoxden and Nether Stowey. Linda and I went there in the spring, the places where Wordsworth and Coleridge wrote the Lyrical Ballads.

It was in the Quantocks that Wordsworth had found hope and faith in life again after his traumatic experience of the Terror and the English declaration of war against France. It was, as Waldo says, where Wordsworth and Coleridge composed *Lyrical Ballads*, the book that marks the beginning of the Romantic movement in English poetry. As Wordsworth and Dorothy found peace and renewal in the Quantocks, in spite of the war with France, so now did Waldo and Linda, though the Second World War against Germany had broken out the year before.

That is surely the 'subtext' of the poem. But in that case, why are Hardy, Keats and Cowper treated at length as poetic exemplars, and why are Wordsworth and Coleridge not even mentioned? What are the other three poets doing in the poem? Neither their presence nor the sequence of their appearance is easily explicable. They are in inverse chronological order, Hardy (born 1840), Keats (born 1795) and Cowper (born 1731). They also go backwards, as it were, through Waldo's own biography, with Hardy in Dorset and Keats at Winchester both within easy reach of him when he was living in Wiltshire sometime during 1946-50; Cowper when he was in Huntingdonshire in 1944; and then (if we wish) Wordsworth and Coleridge in 1940. But there is no obvious objective reason for this order, which must be psychological and spiritual if it is anything other than arbitrary.

Is the whole poem, therefore, simply about his trip to Alfoxden and Nether Stowey with Linda in 1940? If so, the crisis it records and resolves is that of his fierce depression over the outbreak of war. Is the earth 'poisoned'? Was Hardy right to believe that the Mercies could never break onto the hearing of God? But (with Keats) beauty exists; soul-making happens. And Cowper did stand up for slaves and defy the 'anwaraidd gôr' (the 'savage choir'—'wrong' in my version) 'through the secret ways of God.' And like Wordsworth and

Coleridge, Waldo and Linda did find creative happiness in the England of the Quantocks, even in an England that was at war.

This interpretation of the poem fits many of its details, and in fact has a lot to recommend it. It makes the poem conformable to the great thrust of Waldo's poetry against war. It is not, however, a reading that does justice to our sense that 'Tri Bardd o Sais a Lloegr' is overwhelmingly a love-poem, radiant with Linda's presence. The very first line salutes Hardy as 'Pen pencerdd serch,' (supreme love poet) though, to be sure, it qualifies this by saying he is the *pencerdd* of hearts that are severed, across the valley of the shadow of death:

> Supreme love poet through the vale
> That severs heart from heart's delight,
> Whose sleeping God wakes not at all,
> A God seeing neither black nor white.
>
> Behind his house, June on the moor
> And nothing stirs all the long noon.
> What is the quiet waiting for—
> Reedbed and birch, the rush, the broom?
>
> One with the choir of Ages, can
> The Mercies upon His ear break
> And turn to joy? And what is man?
> In the mind of God is he to wake?

At the end, too, Waldo's experience of Linda is said to be 'y fraint o dan y fron' ('the privilege in the breast') and like the sun sends its beams through the valley, clearing the mist and making it bright:

> Your bird song and leaf of the wood
> Sang round about my Linda blest,
> Together sang of her with me
> Who bore the privilege in my breast
>
> As when the sun rises on a hill
> And his gift of warmth reaches down,
> And sets his bright shaft through the vale
> And clears the mist on shining ground.

The whole poem is framed by a cluster of images that occur, subtly changed, both at the beginning and the end. Music is one: the poetic music of Hardy the pencerdd and the singing of the choir of Ages is answered at the end by the birdsong mingled with Waldo's own: 'Together [they] sang of her with me.' Another is less obvious, perhaps: the sleeping God who does not wake through Hardy's long afternoon is answered by the wakening sun rising on the hill. Above all, the 'glyn' ('valley') which in the first stanza is an image of love's tragedy, in the last is warmed and made bright by love, the privilege like the sun.

Surely the poem enacts a spiritual journey through grief: the three poets represent three stages in his coming to terms with his wife's death. Waldo taught in Pembrokeshire until 1942, the year that he married Linda; then he moved to Llŷn. In May 1943 she died after a short illness. A year after her death, in May 1944, he left Wales to teach in various schools in England and did not return until 1950. So England was not simply a country consecrated to Linda's memory, as the poem tells us, it was also where, at least after the first shock of grief, he lived through the loneliness and futility of her absence.

Going back to the beginning of the poem, we have the poet in his misery and bewilderment identifying with Thomas Hardy, the poet of love's idealism betrayed by death, the spokesman of the 'sleeping God'. Grief leads him to ask, will the Mercies ever break on God's ear? Will man wake into the thought of God? Or will this intolerable meaninglessness go on waiting for ever like the quiet host, 'reedbed and birch, the rush, the broom'?

The second section identifies with John Keats in the Winchester harvest fields. Although it was autumn when Keats came there—as it is autumn now, in the poem—still, the great days of his coming were a springtime which will remain for ever in the leaves of his tree—'dail ei bren', the phrase that Waldo was to choose for his own poems.[8] The day like a meadow of beauty, the night a vale ('glyn' again) of soul-making[9]:

> Here, one harvest, your giant came,
> Five foot tall, sure amid mockery,
> And the great days were a springtime
> Will last for ever as leaves of his tree.
>
> How yearned the sun upon its way
> As evening shed its rosy light.
> A meadow of beauty was the day,
> A vale of soul-making the night.

Waldo is surely saying that in the second stage of his recovery, he discovers life's richness again, and that the night of privation can be in fact creative and soul-making.

Thirdly, we have Cowper. Like Cowper, the poet had 'left the herd' like a stricken deer. He had left the close-knit community of Welsh Wales to live and work among strangers in England. But, again like Cowper, he

> from his refuge heard the cry
> Of his brothers betrayed from far—
> Black slaves under an alien sky,
> White slaves in the squalor of war.
>
> And in the silence, by his song,
> By his weakness, alone he stood
> And for man's brotherhood, challenged wrong
> Through the secret ways of God.

It is surely a very different God to the sleeping God of Hardy where this pilgrimage started. The Mercies have indeed broken on His ear and man has woken again into God's mind.

So at the last he thanks England,

> because
> Of your exchange of pleasant speech
> That with me in my great years was.

The context makes it clear that he is primarily thinking of the holiday he spent with Linda in 1940 in the Quantocks. 'Pleasant speech' can certainly, in that context, be taken as a metaphor for the kind of pleasant experiences one has on a holiday; but I do not think a more literal interpretation is ruled out. English was, after all, Waldo's first language, the language of his home as a child. There is abundant evidence of his love for English poetry—not least in this poem. His 'escape' to England for six years after Linda's death—years, incidentally, when most of his greatest lyrics were written —must mean something. And if that is so, then perhaps we can glimpse a wider connotation to 'fy mlynyddoedd mawr,' 'my great years.' Undoubtedly, he is thinking of the all too brief time of his courtship and marriage: but when did those 'great years' end?

So the sun sends its bright shaft through the 'glyn'—often in

Waldo, and indeed in the second line of this poem, carrying overtones of the psalmist's 'valley of the shadow of death'. It is an apt image of consolation, finding renewed life in memories, instead of mere grief and confusion. And it is for the imaginative power to love Linda properly, rejoicing in his memory of her and at the same time facing the challenge of his fellow-poets, Hardy and Keats and Cowper—that Waldo finally thanks England.

Here again, therefore, we find the woman validating and bringing to fulfilment the 'new heaven and the new earth' that Waldo has discovered through dereliction and (in this case) the guidance of his peers. Neither his mother nor Linda were simply sources of comfort to him. In his *cywydd* 'Angharad' remembering his mother he draws a portrait of a Christian quiveringly ready with sympathy and help; but it is not exactly indulgence or consolation that he received from her—

> To us gave, like the sky of God,
> Her anxiety's priesthood.

In 'Y Tangnefeddwyr,' 'The Peacemakers,' he gives equal status to both his father and mother as moral examples to the warring world.

As for Linda, it is the mutuality of their love that he always stresses, how she gave him joy—

> Wherever we were, happiness
> Easy and free about us.

If she was his nest, she was also his heaven (Waldo's favourite bird was surely the skylark!); in his two homes, his helpmate. We remember that in 'Cwmwl Haf,' ('A Summer Cloud)', a home is both

> the slow source of time
> In the cave that is brighter than air

and also

> The house that is out in all weathers.

On the whole, however much the 'awen' (inspiration) uses the subconscious in order to create poetry, Welsh poets write for conscious and socially useful ends. The Welsh tradition is one of light not darkness, consciousness not dream or vision or the archetypes of myth. Waldo's most developed attempt to explore the subjective

29

reality of his relationship with Linda (and therefore of what home meant to him) takes us to the extreme edge of his poetic, where inside and outside, bright cave and new earth, are reconciled in a flux of metaphors and dream-imagery:

> Because of our coming into the quiet room,
> In the timeless cavern,
>
> And because of our going out
> Into the network of roots
> And into orchards of apples,
>
> And because of our going out
> Through the dark veins
> Into the light of bright hearths
> And me, because of my following
> The warm heart,
> My night star,
> My secret of day . . .
>
> And a kiss out to every star restoring
> The deep ocean, the archipelago,
> And two breasts making a new earth,
> Two arms sheltering the country . . .
>
> Because of our coming to the house built strong
> With peace its foundation
> For the joy of our love,
>
> And the world itself coming
> To the deep happiness
> Within sound of the footfall
> Of my gold girl.
> ('Oherwydd Ein Dyfod', 'Because of our coming')

One notices the twofold journey through darkness and light—into the network of roots and the apple orchards, and through the dark veins into the light of bright hearths. Waldo follows the warm heart, 'my night star, my secret of day': 'seren fy nos a rhin fy nydd.' 'Rhin' is a wider word than 'secret'—it can mean something like 'virtue'. One is reminded of Bethlehem, surely. Linda is the star leading him.

In the next lines she becomes almost like God, renewing the whole world, her arms sheltering the countryside ('bro', one's native region). And at the end the world itself comes to the two of them, to 'within sound of the footfall / Of my gold girl'. He suddenly uses a word that generations of love-poets had used before him, 'eurferch',' gold girl', as if to connect his vision with all the love poets of Wales, right back to Dafydd ap Gwilym and beyond. 'Eurferch' is perhaps the most surprising word in the whole poem. In terms of register it seems so different from the rest of the diction, and yet it is absolutely right, the gold picking up both the star and the secret, both Bethlehem and the light of bright hearths.

*   *   *

Waldo was still living and teaching in England for about five years after the war. It was during this period that he wrote most of his poems overtly about the need to safeguard and give dignity to Wales and the Welsh language: 'Preselau', 'Caniad Ehedydd' ('Lark Song'), 'Cymru'n Un' ('Wales One'), 'Cymru a Chymraeg' ('Wales and Welsh'), and 'Yr Heniaith' ('The Old Language'); and perhaps as a sort of appendix, the poem about the sixteenth century Catholic martyrs, 'Wedi'r Canrifoedd Mudan' ('After the Mute Centuries').

There is no doubt what initiated this nationalist sequence. Waldo had always struggled against the way the British military machine tried to take over large tracts of Pembrokeshire countryside. Now, only a year after the end of the Second World War, they threatened it again:

> News of the War Office's plan to take permanent possession of Preseli and to increase its holding there to 16,000 acres became public in the autumn of 1946. Of the 204 farms on and around the mountain, 105 were to be totally requisitioned while the other 99 were to lose part of their land. Half the village of Mynachlog-ddu, including its shop and primary school, would be within the range, as would be 38 sites of archaeological interest . . .[10]

As Ned Thomas says,[11] Waldo, though he was increasingly drawn into nationalist circles through his friendship with D.J. Williams, had not hitherto been known as a nationalist:

31

Waldo had been brought up in a relatively poor and egalitarian rural community with high socialist and universalist principles.

But now, with the War Office trying to take over Preseli, he felt

that the very society which had formed him, which had given him the strength at his back to assert those universal principles, was in jeopardy.

However, while these nationalist poems form quite a self-contained group, it ought to be remembered that Waldo wrote them in the context of other poems, particularly 'Yn y Tŷ', ('In the House'— which I have not translated), 'Cwmwl Haf', ('A Summer Cloud'), and the poem about the Nativity and its effect on Mary and Joseph, 'Y Geni'. What these poems have in common is a sense of the power and strength of home and family life. 'Yn y Tŷ' can perhaps be seen as the fulcrum of both groups, 'written after visiting Mr Mardy Jones at Seven Sisters,' according to the note. It celebrates a home notable for its Welsh culture: nearly every stanza begins 'In the house is . . .' The last stanza reads:

Yn y tŷ mae Gwlad. Daw gwlith
O'i harhosol wybr i lawr,
Mynych ddyfod siriol rith
Yma, o'r blynyddoedd mawr
Yn y tŷ, lle clymir clod
Bardd a beirdd oedd cyn ein bod.

(There's a Nation in the house. Dew comes down from its lasting sky, often a cheerful guise comes here, from the great years in the house, where is knotted the praise of a poet and poets who were before we were born)

It is easy to feel how Waldo's isolation from Wales, the loss of his wife and the home they had made together, turned his thoughts homeward, to Wales as well as to his childhood and the idea of a family. If the threat to Preseli was one constituent of his inspiration at this time, the grief and exile he was suffering certainly formed another. The house that must be defended by effort is one of the main images for Wales in these poems:

It was my window, the harvest and the shearing.
I glimpsed order in my palace there.
There's a roar, there's a ravening through the windowless forests.
Keep the wall from the brute, keep the spring clear of filth.

('Preseli')

Houses are important in Welsh poetry, from Llywarch Hen onwards. Houses, says Saunders Lewis, are where you keep things. But for Waldo (as for David Jones) houses are also important because they have windows. They give access to the order of harvest, the doves, the angels returning:

Let's raise here the old, indestructible stones.
Who are these flying through cloud and sun
Like doves to her windows?

('Yr Heniaith'—'The Old Language')

One of the horrors of modern cosmopolitan existence is that it is a 'windowless' forest where you can't see the brute, only hear and suffer his ravening.

In this century, Wales has often been personified by Welsh poets as a female, a sort of anima-figure: typically she has two aspects, light and dark, princess and prostitute, virgin and hag. This development is typical of a culture in crisis: one thinks of the lamenting women who represent Ireland in the *aislings* of eighteenth century poets like Aogán O Rathaille (Egan O'Rahilly). In Waldo Williams, however, it is not Wales that is personified, but the Welsh language itself, mediating between the despair of the conscious mind and the subconscious strength of the tradition:

. . . she is danger's daughter. Her path the wind whips,
Her feet where they tired, where they fell, those of the lower air.
Till now she has seen her way clearer than prophets.
She'll be as young as ever, as full of mischief.

('Cymru a Chymraeg')

The poetry of this phase was later taken up by the activists of Cymdeithas yr Iaith Gymraeg, the Welsh Language Society. It was quoted and explicated in nationalist summer schools and in court, when they stood trial, almost like texts from the Bible. Cymdeithas yr

Iaith was founded in response to Saunders Lewis's 1962 radio lecture on the Fate of the Language[12], but it was in Waldo's vision that it found continuing inspiration and hope. The poetry of the older nationalists, Saunders Lewis and Gwenallt, had too much tragic clarity to inspire the young. Waldo gave them the joyousness of apocalyptic struggle, in which passive resistance on behalf of the language was linked to anti-imperialism and the campaign for peace.[13]

A poetry as near to propaganda as this has its dangers. Waldo's lapses from grace are few: I can only think of one. The sonnet whose fine sestet I have just quoted, 'Cymru a Chymraeg,' begins perilously close to claptrap:

> Dyma'r mynyddoedd. Ni fedr ond un iaith eu codi
> A'u rhoi yn eu rhyddid yn erbyn wybren cân.

Or, in Clancy's version[14] which is more literal than mine—

> Here are the mountains. One language alone can lift them
> And set them in their freedom against a sky of song.

No such necessary bond obtains between a language and a place. There were languages spoken and sung in the mountains of Wales before Welsh or English were heard of, and with any luck there'll be other languages spoken and sung there long after Welsh and English are heard no more—

> Little words of old, fugitive languages
> That were sprightly on the lips of men
> And pretty to the ear in the prattle of children—
> But no one's tongue will call on them again

to quote Waldo's most popular poem.

*　　*　　*

The forties had represented for Waldo a time of trauma and withdrawal: renewed world war, Linda's death and the six years teaching in England. His only public activity (apart from writing poems) had been the fight to save Preseli from War Office greed. The fifties were to be very different. After he returned to work in Wales in 1950, he decided to stop paying income tax as a protest against the Korean War and against the continuance of conscription into the army. This led to a running battle with the authorities, in the course of which his property was forfeited and in 1960 and 1961 he spent two six-week periods in gaol. This struggle did not end until conscription finally ceased in 1963. In 1953 he joined the Quakers and wrote a pamphlet explaining his decision. In 1959 he was persuaded to stand as a Plaid Cymru candidate in the General Election. He enjoyed the campaign and polled over two thousand votes; but all the same, the thought of Waldo as an M.P. in the lobbies and intrigues of Westminster is mind-boggling. Besides his absent-mindedness and unconventional ways, for a nationalist he had remarkably little liking for the nation state—indeed, national Sovereignty took the place of the devil in his cosmogony.

Meanwhile at least two attempts were made by his friends and admirers to collect his poetry together. The second attempt was submitted to a publisher, accepted for publication and actually in proof before Waldo heard about it. The poet was naturally disturbed by all this effort on his behalf. He forbad publication of the book as it stood: some poems he wanted to include were not in it, some were to be rejected, others to be revised. He had always seemed careless about his poems, leaving them with various friends around the country; but now he took control. *Dail Pren*, his only one-man volume (he had collaborated with E. Llwyd Williams in a book of children's verse), probably owed a lot to the rejected book; but the shape of it, dominated by a rewritten version of his eisteddfod *awdl*, 'Tŷ Ddewi,' and including 'Mewn Dau Gae' ('In Two Fields'), acknowledged ever since as his masterpiece, has considerably more impact.

After the publication of *Dail Pren* in November 1956, there is a definite sense that Waldo relaxed as a poet. He wrote that he 'hoped that *Dail Pren* will be of practical assistance to my nation amid the confusion of this age.' (It is a measure of the difference between Welsh and English poetry that he could say this without posing or being at all pretentious.) Of course, the book contains poems that are free-wheeling, out of range of his pacifist or nationalist ideals: these are chiefly early work or light verse. One almost feels that he failed, for one reason or another, to expunge them. He might have felt that the volume was in danger of being too solemn; or he might just have liked the poems and wanted them included.

But in the poems after *Dail Pren* (which have never been properly collected) the imagination, while still profoundly moral, seems almost free of the desire to be 'of practical assistance' in a time of confusion. They have a lightness of touch, and sometimes a humour that perhaps goes back to his early years as a college wit, but deepened and humanised both by his own experience and by his return to Welsh classical poetry, *cerdd dafod*, as it was still practised by the traditional country poets, the *beirdd gwlad*, the folk or community poets.

Waldo's poetry after *Dail Pren* includes several lyrics, a hymn, a bit of an *awdl* and two fine sonnets, one on Gwenallt the poet, the other, which we have already quoted, on the village where he grew up, Llandysilio-yn-Nyfed.[15] But it is dominated by a series of about half a dozen *cywyddau*, strict-metre poems in couplets, that he wrote in the Welsh classical manner, not about someone or about some thing or idea, but to a specific person at a specific time for a specific reason. At least, all but one are like that; but the very first of the sequence (actually written in 1955, before the publication of *Dail Pren* and very much lighter than the rest) is about a journey he made on his bike to the Gaeltacht, the Gaelic-speaking area in Connemara. Here again, though, there are classical precedents for such a use of *cywydd*. Guto'r Glyn, for example, has a poem on his experiences in England as a cattle-drover, and Tomos Prys on a sea-voyage that included a naval battle.

These cywyddau are an astonishingly varied group: at one extreme the delightful poem celebrating the golden wedding of a cobbler and his wife—it includes an English *englyn* so that even the *Saeson* can join in!

> Fifty years' love above the bog—they made
>   The most of Pebidiog;
>   How did they thrive in Sgeifog?
>   Mid the clay he made the clog.

At the other end of the scale, there's one of the most spiritually meaningful poems he ever wrote, the elegy to his friend Llwyd. It is unfortunate that I have not been able to translate more than one of these *cywyddau*—this same elegy to Llwyd; but Prof. Clancy has kindly allowed me to use his fine version of 'I Isfoel (am y Fodffon)' as it was first called, 'Cywydd Diolch am Fotffon (a gafwyd yn rhodd o law Isfoel).'[16] I am the more pleased to have this poem as it is about the very relationship we've been talking about, that of Waldo's later poetry to the folk or community poets, the *beirdd gwlad*, and through them to the great mediaeval tradition. It is important to know that 'Isfoel' as a place-name means 'below the bare hill,' but that it was also the bardic name of Dafydd Jones, one of an extraordinary family of poets (some dozen in all, over three generations) who lived at a farm called Cilie near Llangrannog in Cardiganshire and who are known as 'Bois y Cilie'. Dafydd Jones was a blacksmith as well as a poet and farmer, so the reference to his anvil is literal as well as symbolic.

CYWYDD DIOLCH AM FOTFFON
(a gafwyd yn rhodd o law Isfoel)

Asb ddudwf ysbyddaden
A dwy fforch yn dod o'i phen,
Hollsyth yw, llaesu o'i thorch
Wedi hoffedd ei dwyfforch,
Ond bondorch ei dibendod
Haeërnin amdani'n dod,
A dant syfrdan odani—
Obry aeth her ei brath hi,
Ti Isfoel wnaeth hoel noeth hon,
Of diangof dy eingion.
Mae daear mwy a'm dyhoel
A'r fforch hardd a'r fferach hoel?
Ffon fawd, diffynnaf â hi
O daw rhaid, rhag direidi.
Dyma'r paladr i ladron.
Rhy wisgi fydd ei fraisg fôn.
Balch wyf mai fi a'i piau,
A cherdd dant yw'r wych rodd dau.
Ysbyddaden awenydd,
Rhinion gwaith ar anian gwŷdd,
A'r clymau fel clymau clod,
Cawraidd dyfiant cerdd dafod,
Uchel gerdd o'i chael o'i wisg,
Cwbwlhâd caboledig,
Camp awenydd, cwmpeini,
Pennaf hwyl pan af â hi.

Dyn wyf i a dan ei fawd
Awen i'w gamre'n gymrawd,
A rhodd hon fo rhyddineb
Isfoel fad yn anad neb.
Eiddigedd cynganeddwr,
Arab deyrn pob trwbadŵr,
Athro dawn, ewythr y De,
Lonnwr calon o'r Cilie.
Gyfaill mawr, dwg fy llaw mwy
Dy fwyn rym hyd fy nhramwy,
Af â hi gennyf hayach
Gamre f'oes drwy Gymru fach.
Ni cheir nant na charn na hollt
Heb drawiad y bedryollt.
Lle'r af i, holl lawr y foel
Hyd arosfa daw'r Isfoel.

THE THUMBSTICK
(a gift from Isfoel)

Asp from a blackthorn giant,
Two-pronged fork thrust from its tip,
Rigid, its coil relaxing
After the vaunt of its fork,
But an iron coil curling
About the base of its foot,
A stunning tooth beneath it—
Its bite's defiance below.
You, Isfoel, wrought this bare nail,
Unforgettable your anvil.
Where's the soil will spill me now,
With comely fork, nail anklet?
A thumbstick, I will at need
Use it to ward off mischief.
Here is the spear for robbers,
Quite brisk will be its stout staff.
Proud am I that it is mine,
Your noble gift is music.

Inspired bard's giant blackthorn,
Mysteries of work on wood,
The knots like a knot of praise,
Poesy's mighty sprouting,
Lofty song won from its woods,
A polished consummation,
Poet's exploit, companion,
Supreme bliss to walk with this.

I'm a man beneath whose thumb's
The muse, his footstep's fellow.
And may this gift be Isfoel's
Facility, none more blest.
Cynghanedd-crafter's envy,
Witty king of troubadours,
Talent's teacher, South's uncle,
Cilie's delighter of hearts,
Noble friend, henceforth my hand
Bears your mild strength while faring.
I will walk, this still with me,
My life's journey through dear Wales,
Not a brook nor cairn nor cleft
Unstruck by these four edges.
Wherever I walk, bare hill,
Till I rest, there's the Isfoel.

It is probably the most traditional poem of any size that Waldo ever wrote—and not just metrically. At least since the fifteenth century poets had written poems to ask for gifts from their patrons, or to thank them for gifts already given—in practice, the two things were often the same: the request was merely formal as the present had already been decided on. These poems would begin with a passage of '*dyfalu*', a series of often fanciful and metaphorical phrases describing the gift; then the giver would be praised and the gift's significance pointed out.

The thumbstick is therefore described as a literal object first: already however, it is an asp, a poisonous snake, whose foot is a 'stunning tooth', 'its bite's defiance.' Waldo will use it not just to walk with but also as a weapon to ward off mischief. We are being prepared for the symbolism of the gift:

Proud am I that it is mine.
Your noble gift is music.
Inspired bard's giant blackthorn,
Mysteries of work on wood,
The knots like a knot of praise,
Poesy's mighty sprouting,
Lofty song won from its woods,
A polished consummation,
Poet's exploit, companion,
Supreme bliss to walk with this.

Without ceasing to be a walking stick—look at the word 'polished'—
the gift has become also the living art of the poet. Both the skill of the
smith and particularly that of the *saer*, the joiner or worker in wood,
were traditional metaphors for the poet's art; the knots in the wood
suggest the knot, 'cwlwm,' a kind of music used for mediaeval
recitation. The image of poetry as sprouting from the wood, itself a
symbol of tradition, is also a traditional idea. There is a kind of wit in
all this, akin to that of metaphysical poetry, but lacking the sense that
the poet is being clever-clever or strained. He is not going beyond
traditional ideas, and he can be confident that the giver—blacksmith
and farmer as he was—would certainly have understood what he was
doing.

So Isfoel's gift becomes the muse beneath his thumb, a talisman for
Isfoel's facility with *cynghanedd*, that is, the strictly organised sound-
play of strict-metre poetry. Celtic poets used their fingers to induce
inspiration, even to compose poetry; so here again there may be a
wittily used traditional image. The poet launches into his praise of the
giver, 'Cynghanedd-crafter's envy . . . Talent's teacher,' and so on.
And then finally Waldo touches on the significance of the gift; for the
first time the traditional patterns are coloured for a moment by more
modern modes of feeling. He says that henceforth his hand bears
Isfoel's mild strength as he walks 'my life's journey through dear
Wales,' 'drwy Gymru fach', literally 'through little Wales.' And that
phrase is Waldo, not the tradition. It conjures up, to those who know
his work, poems like 'Yn Nyddiau'r Cesar' with its 'cenedl fechan',
its 'little nation': the Wales of 'Preseli' or 'Mewn Dau Gae,' a Wales
to be wondered at, a window, but also a house to be protected, a spring

to be kept clear of the ravening beast. What he's implying is that this traditional poetry of Isfoel's, like the thumbstick's iron point,

> Not a brook nor cairn nor cleft
> Unstruck by these four edges,

is his best defence and support for 'dear Wales.'

*   *   *

In his book *Praise above all: Discovering the Welsh Tradition*,[17] A.M. Allchin likens the Welsh poet's traditional habit of writing elegiac *cywyddau* (*marwnadau*) for his friends to the manufacture of sacred icons of the saints in the Eastern Orthodox Church. It is not a comparison which would ever occur to an academic specialist in either icons or Welsh literature, but both are processes in which traditional craftsmanship of a particularly rigorous kind forges self-discipline into creativity. Both achieve a concentration of energy and meaning with the aid of a strict set of conventions. The icon is explicitly and exclusively liturgical, painted and used with prayer, a sacramental vehicle for human intercourse with heaven. Of course, the *cywydd* is none of those things explicitly; but Allchin demonstrates that there is an implicit liturgical function, an agreement on the nature of poetry as praise; that there is, even overtly, an emphasis on the death-defying quality of art; and that (in some poems at least) the death-defiance celebrates a further victory over death, the union of the saints in heaven with those on earth, achieved through the love in the heart of Jesus and his sacrifice on the Cross. He quotes what Nicholas Zernov says of icons, that they are 'pledges of the coming victory of a redeemed creation over a fallen one.'

One of the poems Allchin analyses is Waldo's *cywydd* mourning his friend Llwyd. Allchin is at his best explaining its mystery, the sense of fragility that yet couples an enormous strength of traditional lamentation with intensely personal feeling:

> Mae'r holl iaith os marw yw Llwyd?
> Nid yw brawddeg ond breuddwyd,
> A'r niwl oer ar y waun lom
> Os trengodd ystyr rhyngom.

(Where is the whole language if Llwyd is dead?
A sentence is only a dream
or a cold mist on the barren moor
if meaning has perished amongst us—or between us . . .)

> If Llwyd's dead, what's all language?
> No sentence more than a dream,
> A cold mist on a bare moor,
> If meaning's lost between us.
> Pure God, father of light, bring
> Back to us your bright dawning.
> Your glory is your heart. Love shoots
> From you, up from the saint root.
> Your love's tied above our clay,
> Knots over fall a safe stay.
> In our severance dwell, so we
> Into one House may journey!

'Llwyd' is in many ways a conventional *cywydd*, even in its phraseology—

> Fy hiraethlef ar frithlawr,
> Llwyd, cêl fardd Allt Cilau-fawr.

(My cry of longing on a chequered floor,
Llwyd, hidden poet of Cilau-fawr Wood.)

The icon-like function that Allchin finds is certainly a traditional one, even though some of the turns of thought that illuminate it are those of a great individual imagination widely read in more than one culture. The *cywydd* on the death of a friend I suppose is a renaissance form—there is a splendid sixteenth century example of a professional poet's *cywydd* on the death of a friend (who was also a cleric and a poet), William Llŷn's Elegy for Syr Owain ap Gwilym.[18] It would take a wide knowledge of such poems down to the 20th century to determine precisely how far Waldo is being original, how far he is using the convention to his own ends, and how far he is simply being traditional —

> Ac oddi cartref hefyd
> Aeth cu fab Wythcae o Fyd.

That sounds very much the sort of thing any *cywyddwr* might say. It is the enormity of his key-changes, modulating from the dead man to God, to poetry, to the land, to the mist of death and finally to the three bereaved ones—all within about six or seven lines—that is so extraordinary, even in a form that makes multiple parenthesis a fine art:

> The dear man left Wythcae's world—
> Gave up walking the hill brim
> For two yards in Rhydwilym.
> Oh, where's vision, free created?
> A great wound is a poet's death.
> Raise our race, keep our folk hoard,
> Lift your burden on us, Lord,
> And for the three dear ones, turn
> Mist at the ford to sunshine.

Looking back to the couplet I've just quoted—

> Ac oddi cartref hefyd
> Aeth cu fab Wythcae o Fyd.

(And from home also
The dear son has gone from Wythcae's world)

How far has Llwyd by his life *already* made his home (Wythcae's world) a part of 'yr un Tŷ'—the one House—that is our journey's end, in the husbandry of the neighbourhood of God? Llwyd was both part of the vine and its harvester:

> And the sap of the vine still
> Flowed in him, a sure goodwill.
> Open and mild amongst us, unlost
> He carried home the harvest.

In Rhydaman he had been a shepherd, a good steward, bringing hearts into God's presence,

> The unfailing fullness, God's
> Husbandry of neighbourhood.

'Hwsmonaeth cymdogaeth Duw'—*cynghanedd sain* positively clattering through the dear abstractions into the open water of the mystery.

And from home also he's gone, even from his own piece of 'cymdogaeth Duw', God's neighbourhood. From the very particularised home, Allt Cilau-fawr, Wythcae, the graveyard at Rhydwilym, he has gone. From Rhydaman, Aman ford, from Rhydwilym, Gwilym's ford, the ford at which God has put the mist which the poet prays will turn to sunshine for three dear ones. Suddenly we are in an Arthurian world, a dark age where the way across fords settled the fate of peoples. And this ford is surely in the 'glyn erch,' the vale of dread. Look, already the light is coming though it, breaking on it, 'yn hardd,' 'beautifully':

> Let me greet you, good soul. Glinted
> Light breaks through the vale of dread.
> I keep your balm for always,
> Preaching, that tips summer days
> To sing for ever, 'Blessed
> Are the meek.' A glitter, a glad
> Preaching, a nightingale's tune—
> The grove of night's full of heaven.
> Your music is there. Shine, and
> Spread its gift over the land.

'I have your balm.' The balm of this rich and meek man, the sap of the vine: 'I have/ I will have your balm in memory without fail.' The very top of the summer sings your sermon for ever—'Gwyn eu byd y rhai addfwyn'—white is the being of the gentle ones, blessed are the meek—that is what Llwyd preached, whose 'addfwynder oedd ei fendith,' whose blessing was his gentleness, whose meekness was his blessing; and because Llwyd lived like that, that is the sermon of him that the high summer sings. And then the light changes again, and from the sunlight of Shelley's Adonais—part of the loveliness he makes more lovely—we move to the grove of night and the light of the nightingale's song.

> Ireiddfyd
> Pregeth loyw, pur gathl eos.
> Llawn o Nef yw llwyn y nos.

A green thought in a green shade, isn't it? 'A green world of bright preaching, pure song of a nightingale.' 'Cathl' which the dictionary derives from a hypothetical Celtic 'cantlon' (same root as *canu*) a song, a ditty, a psalm, was a term used by sixteenth century free-metre poets for a lyric; but it is a more celebrated 'cathl' which is directly relevant to the poem. Waldo is thinking of Alun's 'Cathl i'r Eos', the 'Cathl to the Nightingale', one of the most famous lyrics in the language.[19] Alun's poem makes the nightingale a symbol of the devoted wife, soothing her husband after the troubles of the day, and with her self-sacrifice prefiguring the hope of dawn.

So *pregethu* and *canu* intertwine, the bright song of Dafydd's thrush preaching from his thorn, and the singing of Alun's nightingale, full of heaven in the grove of night.

> Ynddi mae d'awen heno

Isn't the *cynghanedd lusg*, the rhythm of it, echoing that line I started with?—'ac oddi cartref hefyd'. He that has left his home has found it. 'In it tonight'—that is, in the grove of the night that is full of heaven— is Llwyd's 'awen', his inspiration or muse, or perhaps his 'music' would be the best way to put it. And then a line which is pure Waldo Williams and virtually untranslatable—

> Tywynna'r fraint, taena'r fro
> (Shine out the privilege, spread it over the land)

though even here the word 'tywynnu' has been suggested by Alun's penultimate line—

> Yn t'wynnu, megis llygad aur,
> Trwy bur amrantau'r borau.

> (Shining, like an eye of gold,
> through the pure eyelids of the morning.)

If one may go back and compare the poem he wrote to the memory of his wife Linda, 'Tri Bardd o Sais a Lloegr,' addressing the English countryside:

> A'th adar cerdd a dail y coed
> Yn canu o gylch fy Linda lon,
> Cydganu a mi amdani hi
> Yn dwyn y fraint o dan y fron

Megis pan gyfyd haul ar fryn
Ac estyn obry rodd ei wres
A rhoi ei baladr gloyw trwy'r glyn
A phuro'r tarth a pheri'r tes.

(Your bird song and leaf of the wood
Sang round about my Linda blest,
Together sang of her with me
Who bore the privilege in my breast

As when the sun rises on a hill
And his gift of warmth reaches down,
And sets his bright shaft through the vale
And clears the mist on shining ground.)

Bird song, privilege (*braint*), light penetrating the vale (*glyn*, used of the Valley of the Shadow) and clearing the mist are common to both poems. 'Yn dwyn y fraint o dan y fron'—reminds us again of Alun's 'Ac os bydd pigyn dan o fron' ('And if the thorn's under the breast— 'o dan y fron' 'under the breast' is not the usual idiom, and in my version I have not translated it literally as the implied quotation would only confuse an English reader). Waldo is probably thinking of the bitter-sweet privilege of having loved Linda and lost her. 'Braint'— privilege—is one of his big words.

Reading 'Llwyd' involves you in experiencing the dead man's life not just as a pattern of moral goodness but as a sacrament, a renewal of grace. The poem 're-members' and re-activates in us God's love that flowed through Llwyd when he was alive. The death-defying quality of art celebrates the victory over death of the communion of saints in Christ. Like an icon, as Allchin would say, the poem is a pledge of the coming victory of a redeemed creation over a fallen one.

*   *   *

It sometimes seems as though Waldo Williams was a throw-back to the great English Romantics, particularly Wordsworth and Coleridge. His mysticism as well as his faith in the brotherhood of all men—his sense, too, of the importance of his poetry to his country—reminds me of them. As we have seen, towards the end of his life he also veered towards a tradition that was even older, that of the classical Welsh middle ages, as that still lived on in the work of the country poets, the *beirdd gwlad*.

And yet of all the great Welsh poets of this century, Waldo seems the most contemporary. He is the patron saint of the Language movement and of Pacifism in our time. His politics of home—the house that is out in all weathers—civil disobedience, waiting for the government to commit injustice, withholding the duties of a citizen towards a state that is seen as unjust—has had more mileage in it than either of the other two politics: that of the day, public meeting and political party, or that of the night, the clandestine quasi-terrorist attack on property. Whether this advantage will continue in Wales is problematic. On a world scale, these Gandhi-like tactics have already brought Communism to its knees. The setback they suffered in Beijing, however, may have been more drastic than at first appeared. The massacre of the student protesters by government troops may well have demoralised such politics for a long time to come.

On a more poetic level (not that the two things can be separated in this of all poets) Waldo appeals to an age which sets 'caring' up as an absolute, which is suspicious of all-male approaches, and for which the threat to the future—to children, to humanity, to the earth itself—is a constant preoccupation. Rapid and seemingly irreversible change breeds anxiety; and Waldo's joy and sense of rightness can move one to tears. As someone once said of Wordsworth, he has a wisdom to offer.

NOTES

[1]Dafydd Glyn Jones suggests in a letter to me that the portrait of Davies is a composite one: 'I'm sure there's a lot of D.J.W. in the "tubby humorist"; it sounds to me like a portrait of D.J., coupled with Waldo's protest.' D.J. is of course D.J. Williams the writer and Plaid Cymru activist, one of Waldo's closest friends.

[2]Cf. Tony Conran: 'Waldo Williams's "Three English Poets and England"', *New Welsh Review*, no. 11 (Winter 1990-91). I have adapted parts of my article to the purposes of this introduction.

[3]It is unfortunate that I was unable myself to translate 'Tŷ Ddewi' for this book. It is written in the so-called 'Mesur Llundain', a combination of two metres, four lines of *cywydd* followed by the four-line *gwawdodyn*. The *gwawdodyn* goes fairly easily into unrhymed four-stress lines—how I normally do *awdl* measures; but I cannot manage to centre the *cywydd* in English verse except in seven-syllable syllabics with a very difficult kind of off-beat rhyme. The combination of these two incompatible prosodies is quite impossible to manage—not just for formal reasons but because you go from comparative ease to extreme difficulty and back again, every four lines. I'm sure there is a way of doing it, but I certainly have not found it.

However, Prof. Dafydd Johnston of the University of Wales, Swansea, has very kindly furnished me with a prose or free-verse translation of the *awdl*, which is given in an appendix. In view of the importance of the poem, I am very grateful for his help.

[4]*Waldo Williams* (Writers of Wales), University of Wales Press, 1975, p. 33. This is confirmed by a note by D.J. Williams on the title page of a draft of the *awdl*. See the standard bibliography, 'Gweithiau Waldo Williams' by B.G. Owens, *Y Traethodydd*, Hydref 1971, p. 315.

[5]Statement of Waldo Williams as a conscientious objector, to the tribunal in Cardiff, 12th Feb. 1942: published in the Waldo Williams number of *Y Traethodydd*, Hydref 1971, p. 254.

[6]There is a remarkable prefiguration of this flight in a poem of 1939, 'Diwedd Bro,' ('End of a Countryside'), expressed in terms of Mabinogion story: as in 'Cwmwl Haf' the collapse of reality is put in mythological terms—

> The mist shower came like a net
> Thrown in a moment down
> By a grey, light-handed thief . . .
>
> Two orphans of the land
> Weeping at all that woe—
> 'Let's leave it now,' he says.
> To England off they go.

It seems to have been written, like 'Daw'r wennol yn ôl i'w nyth' ('The swallow will find her nest'), out of Waldo's concern that the army was taking over so much Pembrokeshire farmland for military purposes.

[7]*Waldo: Cyfrol Deyrnged*, edited by James Nicholas, 1977, p.41.

[8]The poet is quoting Keats' 'axiom': 'That if Poetry comes not as naturally as the leaves to a tree it had better not come at all.' *Letter to John Taylor*, 27th Feb. 1818.

[9]Waldo refers in his notes to Keats' saying: 'This world is a vale of soul making.' (*Letter to George and Georgiana Keats*, 14th Feb.-3rd May 1819).

[10]Janet Davies: 'The Fight for Preseli, 1946', *Planet* 58, Aug./Sept. 1986, p. 4.

[11]Ned Thomas: 'The Waldo Dialectic', *Planet* 58, Aug./Sept. 1986, p. 14.

[12]There is an English translation of the lecture in *Planet* 4, Feb.-March, 1971, pp. 13-27.

[13]For Waldo's poetic strategy and apocalyptic vision in these and other poems, and their relation to the 'myth-making' born of crisis in the Welsh-language community, see Toni Bianchi: 'Waldo and Apocalypse,' *Planet* 44, August 1978. 'The visionary, in the face of seemingly insuperable crisis, must have access to a higher truth in the light of which that crisis can be seen as but a temporary set-back.' Bianchi sees as central to Waldo's poetry this juxtaposition of crisis and apocalypse, and he compares it to such things as the messianic cults of colonial Africa, the 'fantastic optimism' of the millenarian Ghost Dance cult of the Plains Indians, and the Black Zionism of the Jamaican Rastafarians; or in literary terms, to the marriage of mystical and the political in certain Russian writers (Solovyov, Ivanov, Bely, Berdyaev) at the turn of the century, in the Nigerian Soyinka's poem, 'Ogun Abibiman,' and in modern Hebrew writers, particularly Bailik, Fichman, S. Shalom and Avigdor Hameiri. The trouble with Bianchi's very interesting article is that it tends to group all these movements together (and Waldo's poetry) as lost causes before you start. It ignores the fact that the Welsh poet has been the traditional leader and ideologue of his community, and that Waldo's apocalyptic strain, even as a rhetorical device—and it is of course much more than that—actually did succeed. It was a powerful rallying point for language reform and civil disobedience movements, and was certainly a prime factor in creating the uneasy bilingualism we have now. Whether our present Wales would have pleased Waldo is doubtful; but there is no doubt that he is one of its chief architects.

[14]Joseph P. Clancy: *Twentieth Century Welsh Poems*, Gomer, 1982, p. 130 ('Welsh Land, Welsh Language').

[15]The sonnet in Welsh is a thing apart, because it only really became a major form in the twentieth century. As a result, you don't get the shadow of Petrarch hanging over it: there are virtually no love-sonnets in Welsh. One parent was certainly the English romantic sonnet of Wordsworth, Shelley and Keats, with perhaps some Milton for good measure. There are Welsh poets influenced by French and German symbolists and post-symbolists, but on the whole they don't use sonnets; so the Baudelairean sonnet, for example, hardly touches Welsh. On the other hand, the largely rationalist basis of most Welsh poetry— for the most part based on Christian humanism—made the empiricism of Wordsworth and Keats problematic for most Welsh sonneteers. The big exception is Williams Parry, who is almost certainly the finest and most varied of them all, who rebelled against his tradition and the whole chapel-dominated ethos of his time by adopting a more or less empiricist outlook. The other parent of the Welsh sonnet, however, is more unexpected for an outsider,

the native *englyn* tradition. The *englyn* is a four-line mono-rhymed stanza with full *cynghanedd*, often forming a complete poem in itself but sometimes written in sequences or 'chains'. It has been used from the twelfth century onward for a variety of purposes—personal elegy, imagistic description, moral or gnomic reflections, or (very commonly) epigrams of all kinds, comic or serious, including epitaphs on gravestones. It is a form where neatness and metrical skill can make even quite commonplace sentiments enjoyable. Waldo's English *englyn* quoted in the text *infra* will illustrate the form:

> Fifty years' love above the bog—they made
>   The most of Pebidiog;
> How did they thrive in Sgeifog?
> Mid the clay he made the clog.

Like the sonnet the *englyn* tends to be a bi-focal or binary structure: the octave and the sestet in the sonnet, the first two lines (*paladr* or shaft) and the last two (*esgyll* or wings) of the *englyn*. The connexion between the two forms was made explicit by T. Gwynn Jones, very early on, in a tour-de-force—a sonnet in which three *englynion*, with full rhyme and *cynghanedd*, were 'concealed' within the first twelve lines. You have to go to Bach's 'Art of Fugue' where at one point two fugues, one at twice the speed of the other, are going on at the same time, to get anything like the same kind of contrapuntal complexity.

That is exceptional; but Welsh poets generally have tended to take to the sonnet as though it were a kind of extended *englyn*. Waldo's sonnets occupy a special place in his varied output. They are at once very formal and yet warmly humane, intensely allusive and yet, like all his poetry, basically simple and passionate. Waldo was a great poet in both the old strict metres—*awdl, cywydd, englyn*—and in more lyrical modern measures; but the sonnets seem to me to be halfway between the two, strict metres incognito, as it were, in plain-clothes lyrical dress.

(This note is adapted from the introduction to some of these translations that were published in the Sonnet issue of *The Swansea Review*, No. 14, 1995.)

[16]Clancy, *op. cit.*, pp. 136-7. The original can be found in *Beirdd Penfro*, gol. W. Rhys Nicholas (1961), pp. 155-6.

[17]*Praise Above All: Discovering the Welsh Tradition*, by A.M. Allchin, University of Wales Press, 1991. See Chapter 9, 'The Knowledge which Unites: the death-defying quality of art,' pp. 142-157.

[18]Translated in my *Welsh Verse*, p. 213.

[19]See *Welsh Verse*, p. 249 for a translation—the original is in the *Oxford Book of Welsh Verse*, p. 361.

A NOTE ON THE TRANSLATIONS

Waldo is a very difficult poet to translate, for several reasons. He uses an immense variety of forms, derived from both Welsh and English metrics—and on one occasion from Scots; and he uses them fully aware of their significance. Where he got the form from is often an integral part of the meaning of his poems. Sometimes it is possible to suggest this dimension in translation but quite often it seemed pointless to try. This means that the ghost of something untranslated still haunts your version. The easiest poems to do are often ones which scholars and critics find most difficult, like 'Mewn Dau Gae'—'In Two Fields.' This is because the metre is simply there to articulate the content and does not itself work almost as a controlling metaphor. If the translator is able to articulate the meaning—not just the literal meaning of course—that's all that's required of him. He doesn't necessarily have to use rhyme, even if the original does so. But in most of the sonnets, for example, I have found they fall to pieces without rhyme: the fact that they are sonnets is so much a part of their significance that unless the translation suggests 'sonnet-ness' they fail of their purpose. Waldo's use of poetic structures seems to me most like the use that composers from the fifteenth century up to Bach made of other music. They would compose a mass, for example, using the music of a motet—their own or someone else's—as a compositional base. This was known as a 'parody' mass, without any of the mocking overtones the word usually conveys. The significance of the original motet was added to the mass and expected to play its part in the full appreciation of the new music. In this sense many of Waldo's poems are 'parodies'. His *awdl*, 'Tŷ Ddewi', is a parody of Williams Parry; 'Ar Waun Cas' Mael' a parody of Burns; and 'Eirlysiau' ('Snowdrops') a parody of a well-known hymn about the communion of saints.

It might seem that the Burns example, at least, would work in English; but aside from the difficulty of finding rhymes, the Scots metre has never been naturalised south of the Border. Even Wordsworth, who used it several times, failed to make it anything but an interesting tribute to Burns. Waldo makes it completely at home in Welsh and his poem has no overt reference to the Scots master: but actually the ideology of 'A man's a man for a' that'—democratic, community-based optimism typical of Burns—is an added strength, implied in the form, that Waldo uses to resist the War Office and its militaristic ambitions. In this case I have compromised, using Burns' rhyme-scheme but not the iambic base.

Another reason why Waldo is hard to translate is that the poets he is most like in English (in some respects anyway) are the first Romantics, from Wordsworth to Shelley and Keats. Ned Thomas has an interesting essay on this, comparing Waldo to third-world poets who similarly use Romantic modes of feeling as a means of liberation from colonial strait-jackets. However, for a translator into standard English it means that you're struggling all the time with what seem (but aren't) nineteenth century ways of expressing yourself.

A personal difficulty I've had is that I no longer believe in the iambic as a viable English metre, at least as far as my own verse is concerned. Consequently I've found myself substituting a sort of sprung rhythm, based on stress, for the iambic patterning of the original. Dafydd Glyn Jones many times suggested ways of 'mending the metre', quite small emendations which would make it regular; but my own ear always tends to revise away from the iambic, not towards it. There doesn't seem anything I can do about this, except to stop translating iambic poems!

To illustrate some of the problems that arise in translating Waldo Williams, I'm going to take a brief look at 'Eirlysiau', 'Snowdrops'. It is probably the hardest to put into English verse of any poem I've ever done—it's taken me thirty years, off and on, even to get as far as I have. Not that the meaning is difficult to construe—indeed the Welsh has a luminous quality the reverse of obscure. As I've said, its form 'parodies' a very distinctive Welsh hymn where every stanza begins with a repeated monosyllable:

> Braint, braint
> Yw cael cymdeithas gyda'r saint . . .

Waldo begins his three stanzas like this:

> Gwyn, gwyn
> Yw'r gynnar dorf ar lawr y glyn

('The early crowd on the floor of the valley is white, white'—to put it in normal English word order, as the original is in quite usual, if emphatic, Welsh.)

> Pur, pur . . .

> Glân, glân . . .

So one of the troubles translating it is syntactical: duplication for emphasis is not uncommon even in literary Welsh while in English it tends to be relegated to the nursery—'a big, big dragon.' The main reason why Waldo uses this construction, however, is because the hymn does; and English readers won't know the hymn, so the threefold repetition sounds more and more arbitrary and ludicrous. And that's before you get to the threefold inversion of normal English word-order, which the form insists on anyway.

But on a lexical level also, there are problems. I have difficulties with 'early': compare, 'The train's early'—that is, as opposed to being on time—with 'It's an early train'—that is, not a late one. Just which early is an 'early crowd'? and wouldn't English tend anyway to use 'first' in this sort of context—the first snowdrops, the first flowers of the year? Then again, with the 'crowd on the valley floor', it's difficult not to get embroiled with crowds in the very different Valleys of Idris Davies. And the line after that, 'O'r ddaear ddu y nef a'u myn', means literally, 'from the black earth heaven desires' *or* 'claims' *or* 'demands them', but when we speak of heaven doing that sort of thing in English poetry it's usually a death sentence! I saw no way round this, using 'heaven'. One way was to use 'sky' without an article, to personalise it: 'Out of black earth, sky calls them' was one solution I tried.

But above all I had problems with 'white'. Welsh adjectives tend to carry a quite different (and very rich) connotation compared with their English counterparts. All three of the repeated adjectives, 'gwyn' and 'pur' and 'glân', call for special comment.

52

'Gwyn' obviously means 'white', but 'white' is bare of many of the connotations that the Welsh word has. (In older Welsh, I think, there was another word 'ban'; and in modern 'can', which might be more neutral words, like 'white'.) In fact, all three doubled words—*gwyn, pur, glân*—could at a pinch be translated as something like 'holy.' To say 'snowdrops are very white'- or even 'white, white' has nowhere near the emotional punch of 'gwyn, gwyn.' It is in fact a massively obvious observation. In the circumstances I decided that I would move my opening phrase out of centre, into a fringe connotation, 'holy', while making sure that the primary meaning of the Welsh word was in the reader's mind, maybe later in the stanza.

At this point, using 'holy', someone is going to think of the 'holy, holy, holy, Lord God of Sabaoth' of the Seraphim and the mass—not to speak of *Hymns Ancient and Modern*: doesn't this warrant us using a twofold 'holy' at the start of the stanza? The short answer is no, it does not. Three is not two. As an invocation, 'holy, holy' sounds ridiculous and incomplete, while as a phrase describing snowdrops 'holy, holy, holy' would sound blasphemous for it is never used except about God.

'Pur' offered problems too, particularly as I wanted to reserve 'pure' for the third stanza. In any case the purity of the flower didn't seem to be what Waldo was talking about in this stanza, so much as its staunchness under attack. When I looked up 'pur' in the dictionary I found it had a second meaning, 'faithful', which I accepted as a gift from the gods, more meaningful than 'pure' in this context and carrying on the religious subtext.

In the last stanza, the first whiteness that is the snowdrops' song is 'glân'- 'pure', 'beautiful', 'clear'. Later, when the colours separate (as a prism divides white light) it will be like many different fires; but now this song's 'glân-ness' ('glendid') issues from the lips of God as from a poet in the act of fashioning it. In the whiteness of the snowdrops we are as it were witnessing the pure beauty of God's creative act before it differentiates itself into all the variety and colour of his creation. Surely the imagery of the stanza comes from Shelley—for example, in 'Adonais' the many-coloured dome that stains the white light of eternity.

It is worth remarking that this particular poem of Waldo is very much a piece of verbal music. In its eighteen lines there are twenty-seven words rhyming as main rhymes; two instances of *cynghanedd sain*; two of *cynghanedd groes*; and four of *cynghanedd draws*; besides innumerable cases of simple alliteration. People talk of it as having a consummate music. A translation that is lumpish or clumsy will give no sort of clue as to why it exists. It is beautiful or it is nothing.

The problem remains. Why translate a poem like this, if one can only do it by ignoring many of the features which make it so beautiful in the original? I suppose my answer would be that it represents, more than any other, one polarity in Waldo's writing. To miss it out of a representative selection of his work would be almost unthinkable. One just has to try and get it across—to magic into being, in another language and cultural context, something of the purity and loveliness and sheer energy that it offers.

At the stage that I submitted the book for publication, therefore, my translation read more or less like this:

SNOWDROPS

Very holy
That first hosting down the valley.
Out of black earth, sky calls them.
Light buys them from the bed of mould.
Springtime runs untainted in their white.
They wake over high pasture and field.

Very faithful
Pearl faces of the flower—
For all its modesty, like steel
To bear blows on the lovely cheeks
And lead out, before warm weather,
Summer's array. Are there braver than they?

Very pure
Is their song, the primal white.
When the shards of it scatter
Like a myriad fires they'll colour the fields.
But here it is purity, purity springs
From the Poet's lips who fashions the world.

The readers complained, basically, that I was botching the form and impoverishing the meaning. Regretfully I found myself agreeing with them. Perhaps what I'd been doing had nothing to do with translating a Welsh poem. Perhaps I'd been trying to write an *English* poem using as much of Waldo's terminology and ideas as an English poet decently might—an act of plagiary, therefore, not of translation. There is always something not quite right, not quite English, about a good translation of a poem. Perhaps it was that unEnglishness that my version was trying to will away.

There was nothing for it, then, but to start almost from scratch and do the damn thing again, ignoring all my arguments about why it was impossible. I hope that this time I might have got it—no, not right—but at least more Welsh Waldo than English me.

SNOWDROPS

White, white
The crowd's early down the vale.
Out of black earth, heaven calls them.
Light buys them from the bed of mould,
And the spring runs without taint
From their waking over pasture and field.

Staunch, staunch
The pearl faces of the earliest flower—
For all their modesty, like steel
To bear blows on the lovely cheeks
And lead out, before warm weather,
Summer's array. Are there braver than they?

Pure, pure
Is their song, the primal white.
When the shards of it scatter
Like a myriad fires they'll colour the fields.
But here it is purity, purity springs
From the Poet's lips who fashions the world.

EARLY POEMS

1930-36

MOWTH-ORGAN

Rho donc ar yr hen fowth-organ—
   'Bugeilio'r Gwenith Gwyn',
'Harlech', neu 'Gapten Morgan',
   Neu'r 'Bwthyn ar y Bryn'.

'Dwy' i ddim yn gerddor o gwbwl,
   Ond carwn dy weld yn awr—
Dy ddwylo yn cwato'r rhes ddwbwl,
   A'th sawdl yn curo'r llawr.

A'r nodau'n distewi yn araf,
   Neu'n dilyn ei gilydd yn sionc—
Rhyw hen dôn syml a garaf.
   Mae'r nos yn dawel. Rho donc.

MOUTH-ORGAN

Give us a tune on the old mouth-organ—
    'Bugeilio'r Gwenith Gwyn,'
'Harlech,' or 'Captain Morgan,'
    Or 'Bwthyn ar y Bryn.'

I'm not a musician at all,
    But I'd love to see you now—
Your two hands squat on the double row
    And your heel beating the ground.

The notes fading slowly to silence
    Or following so brisk and gay—
Some old simple tune that I'm fond of.
    The night is quiet. Please play.

YR HEN ALLT

Wele, mae'r hen allt yn tyfu eto,
   A'i bywyd yn gorlifo ar bob tu
Serch ei thorri i lawr i borthi uffern
   Yn ffosydd Ffrainc trwy'r pedair blynedd ddu.

Pedair blynedd hyll mewn gwaed a llaca,
   Pedair blynedd erch 'mysg dur a phlwm—
Hen flynyddoedd torri calon Marged,
   A blynyddoedd crino enaid Twm.

Ond wele, mae'r hen allt yn tyfu eto
   A'i chraith yn codi'n lân oddi ar ei chlwy . . .
A llywodraethwyr dynion a'u dyfeiswyr
   Yn llunio arfau damnedigaeth fwy.

O'r hen allt fwyn, fe allwn wylo dagrau,
   Mor hyfryd-ffôl dy ffydd yn nynol ryw,
A'th holl awyddfryd, er pob gwae, yn disgwyl,
   Yn disgwyl awr datguddiad Meibion Duw.

THE ANCIENT WOOD

The old wood, look, is growing again,
  On every side life is flooding back
Though it's been felled, cut down to feed inferno
  In the trenches of France for four black years.

Four hideous years of mud and bloodshed,
  Four deadly years 'mid steel and bomb,
Old years, old years to break Marged's heart,
  Years to wither the soul of Twm.

But look, the ancient wood's growing again,
  The scab is lifting cleanly from the cut . . .
Though governors of men and their inventors
  Contrive more weapons of damnation yet.

O that gentle wood, I could weep tears,
  So silly sooth your faith in human good,
Despite every grief, so eagerly awaiting
  The hour that reveals us Sons of God.

COFIO

Un funud fach cyn elo'r haul o'r wybren,
    Un funud fwyn cyn delo'r hwyr i'w hynt,
I gofio am y pethau anghofiedig
    Ar goll yn awr yn llwch yr amser gynt.

Fel ewyn ton a dyr ar draethell unig,
    Fel cân y gwynt lle nid oes glust a glyw,
Mi wn eu bod yn galw'n ofer arnom—
    Hen bethau anghofiedig dynol ryw.

Camp a chelfyddyd y cenhedloedd cynnar,
    Anheddau bychain a neuaddau mawr,
Y chwedlau cain a chwalwyd ers canrifoedd,
    Y duwiau na ŵyr neb amdanynt 'nawr.

A geiriau bach hen ieithoedd diflanedig,
    Hoyw yng ngenau dynion oeddynt hwy,
A thlws i'r glust ym mharabl plant bychain,
    Ond tafod neb ni eilw arnynt mwy.

O, genedlaethau dirifedi daear,
    A'u breuddwyd dwyfol a'u dwyfoldeb brau,
A erys ond tawelwch i'r calonnau
    Fu gynt yn llawenychu a thristáu?

Mynych ym mrig yr hwyr, a mi yn unig,
    Daw hiraeth am eich 'nabod chwi bob un;
A oes a'ch deil o hyd mewn cof a chalon,
    Hen bethau anghofiedig teulu dyn?

REMEMBERING

Before the sun has left the sky, one minute,
    One dear minute, before the journeying night,
To call to mind the things that are forgotten
    Now in the dust of ages lost from sight.

Like foam of a wave on a lonely seacoast breaking,
    Like the wind's song where there's no ear to mind,
I know they're calling, calling to us vainly—
    Old unremembered things of humankind.

Exploit and skill of early generations,
    From tiny cottages or mighty hall,
Fine tales that centuries ago were scattered,
    The gods that nobody knows now at all.

Little words of old, fugitive languages
    That were sprightly on the lips of men
And pretty to the ear in the prattle of children—
    But no one's tongue will call on them again.

Oh, generations on the earth unnumbered,
    Their divine dreams, fragile divinity—
Is only silence left to the hearts' affections
    That once rejoiced and grieved as much as we?

Often when I'm alone and it's near nightfall,
    I yearn to acknowledge you and know each one.
Is there no way fond memory can keep you,
    Forgotten ancient things of the family of man?

CWM BERLLAN

'Cwm Berllan, un filltir' yw geiriau testun
   Yr hen gennad fudan ar fin y ffordd fawr;
Ac yno mae'r feidr fach gul yn ymestyn
   Rhwng cloddiau mieri i lawr ac i lawr.
A allwn i fentro ei dilyn mewn *Austin*?
   Mor droellog, mor arw, mor serth ydyw hi;
'Cwm Berllan, un filltir' sy lan ar y postyn—
   A beth sydd i lawr yng Nghwm Berllan, 'wn i?

Mae yno afalau na wybu'r un seidir
   Yn llys Cantre'r Gwaelod felysed eu sudd,
A phan ddelo'r adar yn ôl o'u deheudir
   Mae lliwiau Paradwys ar gangau y gwŷdd.
Mae'r mwyeilch yn canu. Ac yno fel neidir
   Mae'r afon yn llithro yn fas ac yn ddofn.
Mae pob rhyw hyfrydwch i lawr yng Nghwm Berllan,
Mae hendre fy nghalon ar waelod y feidir—
   Na, gwell imi beidio mynd yno, rhag ofn.

CWM BERLLAN

'Cwm Berllan, one mile' is the message written
   At the highway end on the old mute sign
Where the narrow lane is stretching
   Between brier hedges down and down.
Dare I risk that way in an Austin?
   So winding and steep, too rough to try;
'Cwm Berllan, one mile,' is clear on the signpost—
   What's down in Cwm Berllan, say I?

Such apples are there, that old Cantre'r Gwaelod
   Never knew cider with juice sweet as theirs,
And when the birds return from the south land
   All the colours of paradise branches will bear.
The blackbirds are singing. And yon, like a serpent,
   The river is sliding shallow and clear.
Every kind of delight is down in CwmBerllan,
The home of my heart is at the lane bottom—
   No, better I don't go down now, for fear . . .

POETRY
FOR
CHILDREN

Selected from *Cerddi'r Plant*
(with E. Llwyd Williams)

1936

Y MORGRUGYN

Ble wyt ti'n myned, forgrugyn,
   Yn unig, yn unig dy fryd?
Gwelais dy ffrindiau wrth fwlch y waun
   Yn gwau trwy'i gilydd i gyd
   Cannoedd ohonyn-nhw!—
   Miloedd ohonyn-nhw!
   Yn gwau trwy'i gilydd i gyd.

Wyt ti ar goll forgrugyn,
   Ymhell o dy gartref clyd?
Gaf fi fynd lawr â thi i fwlch y waun
   I ganol dy ffrindiau i gyd?
   Cannoedd ohonyn-nhw!
   Miloedd ohonyn-nhw!
   Yn gwau trwy'i gilydd i gyd.

ANT

Ant, where are you going,
   Lonely, lonely by the wall?
I saw your friends at the gap in the moor
   Weaving through each other and all—
   Hundreds of them!
   Thousands of them!
   Weaving through each other and all.

Ant, are you lost and lonely,
   Far from your home you crawl?
May I take you down to the gap in the moor
   Amongst your friends and all?—
   Hundreds of them!
   Thousands of them!
   Weaving through each other and all.

BORE NADOLIG

Beth sydd yng ngwaelod yr hosan?
   Beth sydd i lawr yn y droed?
Mae e'n galed, mae'n gorneli i gyd—
   Y peth rhyfeddaf erioed.

Dyma afal, a dyma orens,
   A dyma ddyrnaid o gnau;
A dyma bacyn o siocoled—
   'Rwy'n eu tynnu i maes yn glau.

Dyma rywbeth—beth yw e? Mowth-organ!
   A dyma whisl bren,
Wel, dyma gwpwl o farbls.
   Beth sy gennyt ti, Gwen?

Ond beth sydd yng ngwaelod yr hosan?
   Y peth rhyfeddaf erioed—
Dau ddyn bach bitw â llif draws
   Yn barod i lifio coed.

CHRISTMAS MORNING

What's in the bottom of the stocking?
   What is it down in the foot?
It's hard, and it feels all corners—
   The strangest thing to put!

Here's an apple, and here's an orange,
   It's a bag of nuts that's tight.
And here's a packet of chocolates—
   I can get them out all right.

Here's something—what is it? Mouth-organ!
   And that's a whistle then.
Well, here's a couple of marbles.
   And what have you got, Gwen?

But what's in the bottom of the stocking?
   The strangest thing to see—
Two tiny men with a two-handed saw
   Ready to down a tree.

CHWARAE

Pan fydd yr haul yn twynnu
    A'r gwynt heb chwythu'n gry',
Â Mair a fi a Deio bach
    I'r cae i chwarae tŷ.

Mae'r waliau'n rhes o gerrig,
    Mae'r llestri ar y seld;
Bydd Mair yn feistres trwy'r prynhawn,
    A ninnau'n dod i'w gweld.

Os daw ymlaen yn gawod,
    A ninnau'n yfed te,
Rhaid rhedeg mewn i'r storws fach
    A chwarae mynd i'r dre.

Hen sach o flawd yw'r ceffyl,
    Fe fyddwn yno chwap.
Bydd Mair yn gofyn, 'Siawns am lifft?'
    Cyn dringo lan i'r trap.

PLAYING

When the sun is shining
   And the wind no more than a grouse,
Mair and me and baby Dai
   Go to the field to play house.

The walls are a line of pebbles,
   The dresser has many a cup;
Mair will be Missis this afternoon,
   And we're coming to look her up.

And if it comes on showery
   When the tea we're drinking down,
We have to run to the little shed
   And play at going to town.

An old sack of flour is the pony,
   We're there before you can clap,
And Mair is asking, 'What chance of a lift?'
   And clambering into the trap.

THE SECOND WORLD WAR

Poems published 1938-46

(with a few of uncertain date which belong here)

Y TŴR A'R GRAIG

I

Ôl hen ryfel a welais,
Y cysgod trwm lle cwsg trais,
Tua'r awyr tŵr eofn,
Yn ddu rhag yr wybren ddofn.
Ban a llym uwchben lli
Talgerth yng ngwynt y weilgi:
Ar dalar y wâr werin
Balch ei droed—heb weilch y drin.
Er y chwyldro, ucheldrem
Yw'r syth ei lun. Mae'r saeth lem
O wythi yw byw bŵau?
Mae'r oerfain wayw? Mae'r arfau?
Mae hil orchfygol Gwilym?
Mae'r aerwyr llu? Mae'r iarll llym?

II

Moel gadarn draw, ac arni
Garreg hen. Y graig, hyhi
Ar welw fin yr wybrol fôr,
Maen garw er mwyn y goror,
A llun dan gymylau llwyd
Yn air praff a ŵyr proffwyd.
Câr y maen a'i hadwaeno;
Difalch a thlawd fel brawd bro
Uwch ei ofal, a chyfyd
Ein baich dros rimyn y byd.
A llefair y gair o'r garn
Erys hwy na'r oes haearn.

THE TOWER AND THE ROCK
(opening sections)

I

Left from a war long ago,
Violence sleeps in its shadow,
Up into air, a stronghold
Black into deep sky is bold.
To the seawind, sharp outline,
Beetle-browed above the brine,
Without hawks of war, still stands
On the civilized headland.
Despite all revolution
Stiff is that wide-watching one.
But where are the sharp arrows
From the sinews of yew bows?
Where's the cold thin spear? the arms?
The kin of conqueror William?
Where are the hosts of battle?
The warriors? and the grim earl?

II

Over there's a bare summit,
An old rock, a boulder on it
By the pale lip of the sea,
A rough stone for a boundary—
Under grey clouds a great word
To a prophet discovered.
Those who acknowledge it, the stone
Loves like a fellow dalesman
Humble and poor, yet higher
In its vigilance and care
Raising up above the rim
Of the world, our lives' burden.
That word spoken from the cairn
Outlasts the age of iron.

DAW'R WENNOL YN ÔL I'W NYTH

Daw'r wennol yn ôl i'w nyth,
O'i haelwyd â'r wehelyth.
Derfydd calendr yr hendref
A'r teulu a dry o dref,
Pobl yn gado bro eu bryd,
Tyf hi'n wyllt a hwy'n alltud.
Bydd truan hyd lan Lini
Ei hen odidowgrwydd hi.

Hwylia o'i nawn haul y nef,
Da godro nis dwg adref.
Gweddw buarth heb ei gwartheg,
Wylofain dôl a fu'n deg.
Ni ddaw gorymdaith dawel
Y buchod sobr a'u gwobr gêl;
Ni ddaw dafad i adwy
Ym Mhen yr Hollt na mollt mwy.

Darfu hwyl rhyw dyrfa wen
O dorchiad y dywarchen,
Haid ewynlliw adeinllaes,
Gŵyr o'r môr gareio'r maes.
Mwy nid ardd neb o'r mebyd
Na rhannu grawn i'r hen grud.
I'w hathrofa daeth rhyfel
I rwygo maes Crug y Mêl.

Mae parabl y stabl a'i stŵr,
Tynnu'r gwair, gair y gyrrwr?
Peidio'r pystylad cadarn,
Peidio'r cur o'r pedwar carn;
Tewi'r iaith ar y trothwy
A miri'r plant, marw yw'r plwy.
Gaeaf ni bydd tragyfyth.
Daw'r wennol yn ôl i'w nyth.

THE SWALLOW WILL FIND HER NEST

The swallow will find her nest,
But kinship leaves the fireside.
Calendar of the homestead
Finished, and the family fled,
People letting the land go wild,
From their heart's country exiled.
A poor thing splendour will be
Along the banks of Lini.

Sun sails from noon, but homeward
Plods no more the milking herd.
The yard's reft of cattle, and woe
To the once-lovely meadow.
The sober cows' procession
With their offering, will not come;
Nor in Pen-yr-Hollt you'll see
The sheep come to the valley.

No more a white crowd's sportive
At the turning of the turf—
Foam-white swarm, trail-winged, they know
Far at sea, a field's in furrow.
No one young ploughs now at all,
Sows seed to the old cradle.
To that school of theirs, war's come—
Crug y Mêl field ripped open.

Where's the stable talk, muttered
Lugging hay, the driver's word?
Ended the strong stamp of feet,
Ended the fourfold hoofbeat.
The language dumb at doorway,
Parish dead, no children play.
But winter won't be endless.
The swallow will find its nest.

DAFFODIL

Y cledd gwych ar y clawdd gwâr,
Llyfnwyrdd yw, llafn o'r ddaear,
Arf bro i herio oerwynt,
Er lliw a chân gwân y gwynt.
Mae gwedd rhwng llawer cledd clau,
Antur llu, cynta'r lliwiau
Trwy fwngwl main o'r wain wyw
Tua'r chwedail, torch ydyw;
Prydferthwch bro, deffroad
Melyn gorn ym mlaen y gad.

Twm Dili, bachgen pennoeth,
Yn lle cap myn y lliw coeth.
Wedi'r dasg, wedi'r disgwyl
Mawrth a'i rhydd ym mhorth yr hwyl.
Hir erys yn yr oerwynt
Chwery'r gêm â chewri'r gwynt.
Chwardd y gwydn serch hwrdd i'w gorff,
Bid lawen fachgen, wychgorff.
Mynnai capten mewn cyptae
Ddeng ŵr fel campwr y cae.

Ledia i maes, Ladi Mawrth,
Ymannerch, eurferch oerfawrth,
Ni faidd ond lili wen fach
O'th flaen, ni thyfai lanach.
Atolwg, dwg ar dy ôl
Do mawr yr ardd dymhorol,
Hyd Ŵyl 'Hangel dawelaf
A'i pherl hwyr a'i Ffarwel Haf,
A gwig adfail, gwag ydfaes.
Ladi Mawrth, ledia i maes.

DAFFODIL

A brave sword by tame hedges,
Earth's blade—and sleek green it is—
A district's dare to cold wind,
For colour's sake, stabs the wind.
Comes amid many a quick sword
(A host's venture) first coloured
From a shrivelled sheath, a thin
Throat, a torque, six petals open.
Neighbourhood's grace, a yellow
Horn to face battle and blow.

Tom Dilly, lad bareheaded,
For cap, wants colour instead.
From task, detention's schoolboy,
March flings wide the doors of joy.
He'll play long in the cold wind
A game with the giants of wind.
Laughs despite buffet—Oh, be
Happy, splendid boy's body!
In a cuptie a captain
Would want, like this champion, ten.

Lead onto the field, Queen March,
A greeting, gold girl of March,
That only white snowdrops dare
Before you, or grew purer.
We ask you, lead out again
A year's growth of a garden
Till quiet Michaelmas drees
Its late pearl and its daisies,
Wood's waste and empty cornfield.
Lady March, lead on the field!

DIWEDD BRO

Rhoed un dan lanw'r môr
  A saith a wnaed yn weddw
Heb derfysg wrth eu dôr
  Na malltod gwyliwr meddw.

Daeth cawod niwl fel rhwyd
  A deflir funud awr,
A'r lleidr ysgafnllaw llwyd
  O'r Foel i'r Frenni Fawr.

Taflwyd ei milmil magl
  A chwim fu'r miragl maith.
Ildiodd saith gantref hud
  Eu hysbryd, gyda'u hiaith.

Heb derfysg wrth eu dôr
  Rheibiwyd cartrefi gwŷr.
Hyd hyfryd lannau'r môr
  Mae llongau meibion Llŷr?

Pan ddaeth y golau claer
  Nid oedd na chaer na chell.
Cyn dristed oedd y saith
  Â'r paith anhysbys pell.

Na chlybu acen bêr,
  Nas gwelodd neb ar hynt
Ond haul a lloer a sêr
  A'r di-greëdig wynt.

A'r ddau amddifad bro
  Dan dristyd hwnt i'r deigr,
Ebr ef, 'Awn ymaith dro',
  Ac aethant, parth â Lloegr.

THE END OF A COUNTRYSIDE

One was put under the tide,
    And seven were widowed here—
No tumult battered the gate,
    No watchman spoilt with beer.

The mist shower came like a net
    Thrown in a moment down
By a grey, light-handed thief
    From Foel to Frenni Fawr.

Its myriad-mesh was thrown
    And swift was the tedious wonder—
With their magic, with their language,
    Seven cantrefs went under.

No tumult battered the gate
    But homes were ravaged here.
On the seashore, where, O where
    Are the boats of the sons of Llŷr?

When the light cleared at last
    There was neither fort nor fane.
As wretched were the seven
    As the far uncertain plain—

The prairie that hears no speech,
    And sees no one go by
But sun and moon and stars
    Along a windy sky.

Two orphans of the land
    Weeping at all that woe—
'Let's leave it now,' he says.
    To England, off they go.

O BRIDD

Hir iawn, O Bridd, buost drech
Na'm llygaid; daeth diwedd hir iawn,
Mae dy flodau coch yn frech,
Mae dy flodau melyn yn grawn.
Ni cherddaf. Nid oes tu hwnt,
Cerddodd dy dwymyn i'm gwaed,
Mi welais y genau brwnt
Yn agor a dweud, Ho Frawd,
Fy mrawd yn y pydew gwaed
Yn sugno'r wich trwy'r war,
Fy mrawd uwch heglau di-draed,
Bol gwenwyn rhwyd y cor.
A phwy yw hon sy'n lladd
Eu hadar yn nwfn y gwrych,
Yn taflu i'r baw'r pluf blwydd,
I'w gwatwar ag amdo gwych?
Ein mam, sy'n ein gwthio'n ein cefn,
Yn mingamu arnom trwy'r ffenestr,
Yn gweiddi, Ho dras, I'r drefn,
A chrechwenu uwchben y dinistr.

O bridd, tua phegwn y de
Y mae ynys lle nid wyt ti,
Un llawr o iâ glas yw'r lle,
A throed ni chyrhaedda, na chri,
I'w pherffaith ddiffeithwch oer,
Ond suo'r dymestl gref
A'r un aderyn ni ŵyr
Dramwyo diffeithwch ei nef,
Lle mae'r nos yn goleuo'r niwl
A'r niwl yn tywyllu'r nos,
Harddach nag ydoedd fy haul
Mabol ar ryddid fy rhos
Er chwipio'r gwyntoedd anghenedl
Ar wyneb di-ïau yr iâ

O SOIL OF THE EARTH

A long time, soil of the earth,
You've been stronger than my sight.
That long time is ended.
Your red flowers are pox,
Your yellow flowers pus.
I'll not move. I've nowhere to go.
Your fever has moved to my blood.
I've seen the filthy maw
Open and say, 'Ho, brother'—
In the blood pit, my brother's
Squeal sucked through his nape,
Legs and no feet, my brother,
Poisoned, snared by a spider.
And who is it slaughters
Their birds in the deep hedge,
Throws to the dirt a year's feathers,
Mocks it like a brilliant shroud?
She pushes us behind, our mother.
She grimaces through the window.
Shouts, 'Ho, people, providence!'
She cackles over destruction.

Soil, towards the South Pole
Is an island where you're not.
A floor of blue ice—
Foot will not reach, nor cry,
Its cold, perfect desert.
Only the blizzard howls.
No bird knows the to-froing,
The wilderness of its sky,
As night lightens mist
And mist darkens night.
More beautiful than the sun
Of my childhood on the moors,
Though whipped by the unbegotten winds
On the sinewless ice

A churo'r cesair dianadl
Heb wneuthur na drwg na da.
Tu hwnt i Kerguelen mae'r ynys
Lle ni safodd creadur byw,
Lle heb enw na hanes,
Ac yno yn disgwyl mae Duw.

By breathless hailstones
Neither evil nor good.
Beyond Kerguelen is that island
Without living creature,
Or story, or name.
There, God's waiting.

BRAWDOLIAETH

Mae rhwydwaith dirgel Duw
Yn cydio pob dyn byw;
Cymod a chyflawn we
Myfi, Tydi, Efe.
Mae'n gwerthoedd ynddo'n gudd,
Ei dyndra ydyw'n ffydd;
Mae'r hwn fo'n gaeth yn rhydd.

Mae'r hen frawdgarwch syml
Tu hwnt i ffurfiau'r Deml.
Â'r Lefiad heibio i'r fan,
Plyg y Samaritan.
Myfi, Tydi, ynghyd
Er holl raniadau'r byd—
Efe'n cyfannu'i fyd.

Mae Cariad yn dreftâd
Tu hwnt i Ryddid Gwlad.
Cymerth yr Iesu ran
Yng ngwledd y Publican.
Mae concwest wych nas gwêl
Y Phariseaidd sêl.
Henffych y dydd y dêl.

Mae Teyrnas gref, a'i rhaith
Yw cydymdeimlad maith.
Cymod a chyflawn we
Myfi, Tydi, Efe,
A'n cyfyd uwch y cnawd.
Pa werth na thry yn wawd
Pan laddo dyn ei frawd?

BROTHERHOOD

Each man alive is knit
Within God's secret net;
The full web's unity
Of I, Thou, He.
What we're worth is hid in it.
Its tension is faith. He
Who is caught in it is free.

Brotherhood old and simple
Is more than all the Temple.
Where the Levite walks on
Bends the Samaritan.
I and Thou, despite
The world's divided plight—
One world he unites.

Inheritance even above
Our Liberty is Love.
Jesus comes, a guest
To the publican's feast.
That splendid victory
Pharasaic zeal can't see.
Hail to the day shall be!

A strong kingdom, where to win
Is suffering with and in
The full web's unity
Of I, Thou, He,
That transcends flesh altogether.
What value ends up other
Than mocked, if man kills his brother?

Y TANGNEFEDDWYR

Uwch yr eira, wybren ros,
   Lle mae Abertawe'n fflam.
Cerddaf adref yn y nos,
   Af dan gofio 'nhad a 'mam.
Gwyn eu byd tu hwnt i glyw,
Tangnefeddwyr, plant i Dduw.

Ni châi enllib, ni châi llaid
   Roddi troed o fewn i'w tre.
Chwiliai 'mam am air o blaid
   Pechaduriaid mwya'r lle.
Gwyn eu byd tu hwnt i glyw,
Tangnefeddwyr, plant i Dduw.

Angel y cartrefi tlawd
   Roes i 'nhad y ddeuberl drud:
Cennad dyn yw bod yn frawd,
   Golud Duw yw'r anwel fyd.
Gwyn eu byd tu hwnt i glyw,
Tangnefeddwyr, plant i Dduw.

Cenedl dda a chenedl ddrwg—
   Dysgent hwy mai rhith yw hyn,
Ond goleuni Crist a ddwg
   Ryddid i bob dyn a'i myn.
Gwyn eu byd, daw dydd a'u clyw,
Dangnefeddwyr, plant i Dduw.

Pa beth heno, eu hystâd,
   Heno pan fo'r byd yn fflam?
Mae Gwirionedd gyda 'nhad
   Mae Maddeuant gyda 'mam.
Gwyn ei byd yr oes a'u clyw,
Dangnefeddwyr, plant i Dduw.

THE PEACEMAKERS

Rose-red sky above the snow
   Where bombed Swansea is alight,
Full of my father and mother I go,
   I walk home in the night.
They are blest beyond hearing,
Peacemakers, children of God.

Neither, within their home, abuse
   Nor slander could be found.
Mam would look for an excuse
   For the biggest scoundrels round.
They are blest beyond hearing,
Peacemakers, children of God.

It was the angel of poor homes
   Gave my father two rich pearls:
Brotherhood the mission of man,
   God's largesse the invisible world.
They are blest beyond hearing,
Peacemakers, children of God.

Nation good or nation bad
   (So they taught) is fantasy.
In Christ's light is freedom had
   For any man that would be free.
Blest, the day dawns that will hear them,
Peacemakers, children of God.

What is their estate tonight,
   Tonight, with the world ablaze?
Truth is with my father yet,
   Mother with forgiveness stays.
The age will be blest that hears them,
Peacemakers, children of God.

Y MILWR

Ei wobr yn fach: wybren faith,
Gwely pell ar gil y paith,
A'i Gymru fyth dan gamraith.

THE SOLDIER

Small his prize: a tedious sky,
A far bed on a patch of prairie,
And Wales, his country, always wronged.

AR WEUN CAS' MAEL

Mi rodiaf eto Weun Cas' Mael
A'i pherthi eithin, yn ddi-ffael,
Yn dweud bod gaeaf gwyw a gwael
   Ar golli'r dydd.
'Daw eto'n las ein hwybren hael'
   Medd fflam eu ffydd.

A heddiw ar adegau clir
Uwch ben yr oerllyd, dyfrllyd dir
Dyry'r ehedydd ganiad hir,
   Gloywgathl heb glo,
Hyder a hoen yr awen wir
   A gobaith bro.

O! flodau ar yr arwaf perth,
O! gân ar yr esgynfa serth—
Yr un melystra, trwy'r un nerth,
   Yr afiaith drud
O'r erwau llwm a gêl eu gwerth
   Rhag trem y byd.

O! Gymru'r gweundir gwrm a'r garn,
Magwrfa annibyniaeth barn,
Saif dy gadernid uwch y sarn
   O oes i oes.
Dwg ninnau atat: gwna ni'n ddarn
   O'th fyw a'th foes.

Yn dy erwinder hardd dy hun
Deffroit gymwynas dyn â dyn,
Gwnait eu cymdeithas yn gytûn—
   A'th nerth o'u cefn,
Blodeuai, heb gaethiwed un,
   Eu haraf drefn.

ON WEUN CAS' MAEL

I'll walk once more on Weun Cas' Mael—
And bushes of gorse tell the tale,
Sick withered winter without fail
    Is losing the day.
'Our kindly sky will be blue in a while,'
    Flaming, they say.

Even today, over the drear
Dank moorland, when a moment's clear
A skylark gives its confident cheer,
    Zestful and strong,
Inspiring hope in the country near,
    Unlocks bright song.

Oh, blossom on the roughest tree,
Oh, song on the steep, wild and free—
One sweet from the one strength, to be
    The brave delight
Of bare acres the world can't see
    Or value right.

Wales of dark moorland and stone,
Nurse of the mind that stands alone,
From age to age your strength's been shown
    And still it stays.
Bring us to share in, O make known
    Your life, your ways!

The lovely severity you show
Woke favour of man with man, to grow
A company all one, and so
    By you empowered,
Knowing no slavery, their slow
    Order flowered.

Dwg ni yn ôl. Daw'r isel gur
Dros Weun Cas' Mael o'r gaethglud ddur:
Yng nghladd Tre Cŵn gwasnaetha gwŷr
 Y gallu gau.
Cod ni i fro'r awelon pur
 O'n hogofâu.

Fel i'r ehedydd yn y rhod
Dyro o'th lawr y nwyf a'r nod,
Dysg inni feithrin er dy glod
 Bob dawn a dardd.
A thrwy dy nerth rho imi fod
 Erot yn fardd.

From steel captivity, low hurt
Crosses Cas' Mael. O save us yet!
Men serve the false power in the pit
    Of dark Tre Cŵn.
To the pure breezes, raise us out
    Of the cave's tomb!

As the lark gives from your ground
Point and zest in his circling round,
Your praise let each gift teach to sound,
    Nurture and grow it,
And grant me, Wales, that I be found,
    For your sake, poet.

LINDA

Hi fu fy nyth, hi fy nef,
Fy nawdd yn fy nau addef,
Ei chysur, yn bur o'i bodd,
A'i rhyddid, hi a'u rhoddodd.
Hi wnaeth o'm hawen, ennyd,
Aderyn bach uwch drain byd.
Awel eithro, haul ei threm,
Hapusrwydd rhwydd lle'r oeddem.
Fy nglangrych, fy nghalongref,
Tragyfyth fy nyth, fy nef.

Mehefin 1943

98

LINDA

My nest, my heaven she was,
In my two homes my succour.
Of her own will, her freedom
And her comfort, she gave them.
Made, that while, my inspiration—
A bird above the world's thorns.
Like the breezes her footstep,
Like the sun the sight of her.
Wherever we were, happiness
Easy and free about us.
My clear curl, my strong heart then,
Always, my nest, my heaven.

June 1943

DAN Y DYFROEDD CLAEAR

Dan y dyfroedd claear
Huna'r gwaed fu'n dwym
Wele, fawrion daear,
Rai a aeth o'ch rhwym.
Wrth eich gwŷs a'ch gorfod
Dygwyd hwy o'u bro.
Rhyddid mawr di-ddarfod
Gawsant ar y gro.

Gwyn a du a melyn
Dan y môr ynghyd
Ni bydd neb yn elyn
Yn eu dirgel fyd.
Dan y dyfroedd claear
Cawsant eang ddôr.
Wele, fawrion daear,
Gariad fel y môr.

UNDER THE GENTLE WATERS
after one of the great battles of the Pacific

Under the gentle waters
Sleeps the blood once warm,
See, ye great and mighty,
Those beyond your harm.
At your beck and summons
They were torn from home,
Great and endless freedom
Got from sand and stone.

White and black and yellow
That the seas enfold—
No one is an enemy
In that secret world.
Under gentle waters
The gate is wide and free.
See, ye great and mighty,
Love that's like the sea.

Y PLANT MARW

Dyma gyrff plant. Buont farw yn nechrau'r nos.
Cawsant gerrig yn lle bara, yn syth o'r ffyn tafl.
Ni chawsant gysgod gwal nes gorwedd yn gyrff.
Methodd yr haul o'r wybr â rhoddi iddynt ei wres,
Methodd hithau, eu pennaf haul, a'i chusan a'i chofl,
Oherwydd cerrig y byd, oherwydd ei sarff.

Gwelwch fel y mae pob ystlys yn llawer rhwgn;
Gwelwch feined eu cluniau a'u penliniau mor fawr,
Dryswch i'w deall oedd methu eu 'Brechdan, mam'.
Aeth pylni eu trem yn fin i'r fron roesai'i sugn.
Ond yn ofer y canai iddynt yn hir ac yn hwyr
Rhag brath anweledig y sarff. Buont farw mewn siom.

Dyma gyrff plant. Gwyn a du a melyn. Mae myrdd.
Llithra'r cawr gorffwyll yn sarffaidd heb si, i bob gwlad.
Lle tery ei oerdorch ef rhed rhyndod trwy'r awyr.
O, gan bwy cafodd hwn hawl ar y ddaear werdd?
Gan seren pob gwallgof, lloer y lloerig: 'Rhaid! Rhaid!'
Gwae bawb sydd yn ffaglu'r seren sy'n damnio'r ddaear.

THE DEAD CHILDREN

Look, bodies of children. Dead at nightfall.
For bread they'd stones, straight from the sling.
No wall sheltered them, till they lay corpses.
The sky's sun—nor she, their best sun of all
With cuddle or kiss—could not warm them,
Because of the stones of the world, because of its snake.

See how their flanks are so scored,
Their thighs are thin, their knees so big!
Perplexity, how their 'Sandwich, mum' failed.
Their dulled looks like a knife went to the breast that gave suck,
But against the snake's invisible bite, long and late
In vain she sang to them. They died disappointed.

Look, children. White. Black. Yellow. A myriad.
He slithers to every country. Monster of madness,
His cold coil strikes, through the air quivers.
Where got this thing its claim on the green world?
From the star of every insanity, the lunatic moon:
                              'Necessity! Necessity!'
Woe all who flame that star, damning the earth.

CÂN BOM

Chwalwr i'r Chwalwr wyf.
Mae'r Codwm yn fy nghodwm.
Ofod, pa le mae Pwrpas
A'i annedd, Patrwm?

Cynllunia fi, ymennydd noeth.
Gwnewch fi, dim-ond dwylo
Dim-ond ystwythder ifanc
Caria fi yno.

Distaw y mae fy meistr
Yn datod cwlwm calon.
Aruthr y deuaf i
Yr olaf o'i weision.

Ef yw'r pryf yn y pren,
Gwahanglwyf y canghennau.
Mi a'u hysgubaf i dân
Ecstasi angau.

BOMB SONG

I shatter him who shatters.
The Fall is in my falling.
Space, where is Purpose
With Pattern, its dwelling?

Design me, naked brain.
Mere hands, O make me.
There, you young
Suppleness, take me.

Calm, calm my master
Looses heart's knot.
Most dire of his servants,
I come last of all.

He is worm in the wood,
Leprosy of branches
That I sweep to the fire
Of the frenzy of death.

ACKNOWLEDGE

Poems published 1946-56

(before the publication of *Dail Pren*)

ADNABOD

Rhag y rhemp sydd i law'r dadelfennwr
A gyll, rhwng ei fysedd, fyd,
Tyrd yn ôl, hen gyfannwr,
Ac ymestyn i'n hachub ynghyd.
Cyfyd pen sarffaidd, sinistr
O ganol torchau gwybod.
Rhag bradwriaeth, rhag dinistr,
Dy gymorth O! awen Adnabod.

Y mae rhin cydeneidiau'n ymagor
O'u dyfnder lle delych yn hael.
Mae ein rhyddid rhagor
Yn nhir dy ddirgelwch i'w gael.
Ti yw'r wyrth. Ti yw'r waddol
A geidw bob cymdeithas yn werdd.
Ti yw'r un gell dragwyddol
Yn ymguddio yng nghnewyllyn pob cerdd.

Dy dystion yw'r sêr, i'w hamseriad
Yn treiglo eu cylchoedd trwy'r cant—
Rhai clir fel cof cariad
A sicr fel dychymyg y sant.
Ti fo'n harf. Ti fo'n hynni.
Ti sy'n dangos y ffordd ddiffuant.
Tosturi rho inni
A'th nerth ar esgynfa maddeuant.

Ti yw'n hanadl. Ti yw ehedeg
Ein hiraeth i'r wybren ddofn.
Ti yw'r dwfr sy'n rhedeg
Rhag diffeithwch pryder ac ofn.
Ti yw'r halen i'n puro.
Ti yw'r deifwynt i'r rhwysg amdanom.
Ti yw'r teithiwr sy'n curo.
Ti yw'r tywysog sy'n aros ynom.

ACKNOWLEDGE

From a world lost through the fingers
Of those who dissect and sever,
Stretch, old wholeness-bringer,
Reach out, save us together.
A snake head, sinister, rises
Out of the coils of knowledge—
Against treason, against destruction,
Help us, O muse Acknowledge!

Soul opens to soul its secret
From the depths where you are kind.
In the land of your mystery
Henceforth our freedom we'll find.
Acknowledge, you're miracle. You're dowry
That keeps community green.
Hid cell of everlastingness
That all poems mean.

Stars are your witnesses, the timing
Orbits turn as you acquaint—
Clear as love's memory, and sure as
The imagination of a saint.
Acknowledge, be our weapon, be energy.
You show sincerity's way.
Give to us mercy, and strength
On the climb of forgiveness to stay.

You're our breath. You're our hiraeth's
Flight to the deep sky.
Against desert of anxiety and fear
You're water flowing by.
You're the salt to make us pure.
You're the blast to the pomps of state.
You're the traveller who knocks,
And within us, you're the Prince who waits.

Er gwaethaf bwytawr y blynyddoedd
Ti yw'r gronyn ni red i'w grap,
Er dyrnu'r mynyddoedd,
Er drysu'n helynt a'n hap.
Ti yw'r eiliad o olau
Sydd â'i naws yn cofleidio'r yrfa.
Tyr yr Haul trwy'r cymylau—
Ti yw Ei baladr ar y borfa.

Despite the devourer of years
You're the grain that's not to his grip,
Despite the threshing of mountains
And the tangle of chance let rip.
You are the moment of light
That embraces the way we pass.
The Sun breaks through the clouds—
You're His radiance on the grass.

PRESELI

Mur fy mebyd, Foel Drigarn, Carn Gyfrwy, Tal Mynydd,
Wrth fy nghefn ym mhob annibyniaeth barn.
A'm llawr o'r Witwg i'r Wern ac i lawr i'r Efail
Lle tasgodd y gwreichion sydd yn hŷn na harn.

Ac ar glosydd, ar aelwydydd fy mhobl—
Hil y gwynt a'r glaw a'r niwl a'r gelaets a'r grug,
Yn ymgodymu â daear ac wybren ac yn cario
Ac yn estyn yr haul i'r plant, o'u plyg.

Cof ac arwydd, medel ar lethr eu cymydog.
Pedair gwanaf o'r ceirch yn cwympo i'w cais,
Ac un cwrs cyflym, ac wrth laesu eu cefnau
Chwarddiad cawraidd i'r cwmwl, un llef pedwar llais.

Fy Nghymru, a bro brawdoliaeth, fy nghri, fy nghrefydd,
Unig falm i fyd, ei chenhadaeth, ei her,
Perl yr anfeidrol awr yn wystl gan amser,
Gobaith yr yrfa faith ar y drofa fer.

Hon oedd fy ffenestr, y cynaeafu a'r cneifio.
Mi welais drefn yn fy mhalas draw.
Mae rhu, mae rhaib drwy'r fforest ddiffenestr.
Cadwn y mur rhag y bwystfil, cadwn y ffynnon rhag y baw.

PRESELI

Wall round my boyhood, Foel Drigarn, Carn Gyfrwy, Tal Mynydd,
At my back in all independence of mind,
My ground, from Witwg to Wern and down to Yr Efail the Smithy
Where the sparks flew that are older than iron.

And on farmyards, on hearths of my people—
Breed of wind, rain and mist, flag iris and heather,
With the earth and the sky they wrestled and carried,
Bent as they were, reached and gave children the sun.

Both memory and sign. Reapers on a neighbour's slope.
Four swathes of oats felled at each sweep
On the one swift way. Then, straightening their backs,
A giant's laugh to the clouds, one shout, four voices.

My Wales, brotherhood's country, my cry, my creed,
Only balm to the world, its mission, its challenge,
Pearl of the infinite hour that time gives as pledge,
Hope of the tedious race on the short winding way.

It was my window, the harvest and the shearing.
I glimpsed order in my palace there.
There's a roar, there's a ravening through the windowless forests.
Keep the wall from the brute, keep the spring clear of filth.

CANIAD EHEDYDD

Ymrôf i'r wybren
Yn gennad angen
Fel Drudwy Branwen
    Yn nydd cyfyngder.
Codaf o'r cyni
A'm cân yn egni
Herodr goleuni
    Yn yr uchelder.

Disgyn y gloywglwm
Hyd lawer dyfyngwm
Lle rhoddodd gorthrwm
    Gleisiau ar geinder.
Gwiwfoes yr oesoedd
Hardd yr ynysoedd,
Branwen cenhedloedd
    Codaf i'w hadfer.

Bydd mwyn gymdeithas,
Bydd eang urddas,
Bydd mur i'r ddinas,
    Bydd terfyn traha.
Eu Nêr a folant
Eu hiaith a gadwant,
Eu tir a gollant
    Ond gwyllt Walia.

LARK SONG

I give myself skyward
As heartache's envoy
Like Branwen's starling
   In a day of woe.
Rising from anguish
My song's endeavour
A herald of light
   To the height I go.

The bright knot alighting
On many deep valleys
Where fineness is bruised on
   Oppression's rack:
Age-old good custom,
Beauty of the islands,
A Branwen of nations
   I fly to bring back.

There'll be gentle community,
There'll be broad dignity,
There'll be walls to the city,
   Arrogance shall fail.
Their Lord they will praise,
Their language they will keep,
Their land they will lose
   Except wild Wales.

CWMWL HAF

'Durham', 'Devonia', 'Allendale'—dyna'u tai
A'r un enw yw pob enw,
Enw'r hen le a tharddle araf amser
Yn yr ogof sy'n oleuach na'r awyr
Ac yn y tŷ sydd allan ymhob tywydd.

Bwrw llond dwrn o hedyddion yma a thraw
I alw cymdeithion y dydd,
Yn eu plith yr oedd anrhydedd llawer llinach.
Henffych i'r march mawr teithiol dan ei fwa rhawn,
A'i gerddediad hardd yn gywydd balchder bonedd,
Ninnau'n meddwl mai dangos ei bedolau yr oedd.

Ac wele i fyny o'r afon
Urddas wâr, urddas flith, fel y nos,
Yn plygu'r brwyn â'i chadair
Ac yn cario'r awyr ar ei chyrn.
Ac yn ein plith ni, arglwyddi geiriau,
                              yr oedd rhai mwy
Na brenhinoedd hanes a breninesau.
Ym mhob tywydd diogelwch oedd y tywydd.
Caredigrwydd oedd y tŷ .

Unwaith daeth ysbryd cawr mawr i lawr
Trwy'r haul haf, yn yr awr ni thybioch,
Gan daro'r criw dringwyr o'u rhaffau cerdd,
Nid niwl yn chwarae, na nos yn chwarae,
Distawrwydd llaith a llwyd,
Yr un sy'n disgwyl amdanom,
Wele, fe ddaeth, heb ddod.
Caeodd y mynyddoedd o bobtu'r bwlch,
Ac yn ôl, yn ôl
Fel blynyddoedd pellhaodd y mynyddoedd
Mewn byd oedd rhy fud i fyw.
Tyfodd y brwyn yn goed a darfod amdanynt
Mewn byd sy'n rhy fawr i fod.

A SUMMER CLOUD

'Durham,' 'Devonia,' 'Allendale'—those are their houses
And every name is the same name,
Name of the old place and the slow source of time
In the cave that is brighter than air,
The house that is out in all weathers.

A fistful of larks thrown here and yonder
To summon the playmates of day
And among them a much-pedigreed notable—
Greet the great travelling stallion, his mane a sprung bow,
His action lovely, a strictness, a pride of lineage—
We thought he was showing off, too big for his boots!

And see, up from the river
A mildness, a milch dignity, like night
Bending the rushes with her udders
And on her horns carrying the sky.
And among us, lords of words, were those
Greater than history-kings and queens.
In every weather, security was the weather.
Love and kindness was the house.

A spectre of a huge giant came down once
Through the summer sun, in an hour you'd not think it—
Struck from their ropes of music the mob of climbers,
No play of mist, neither play of night,
A dank and grey stillness,
The one that is waiting for us—
No coming at all, look, it just came.
Mountains closed on each side of the gap,
And back, back
Like years, mountains moved further and further
In a world too silent for life.
The rushes grew into trees and ended
In a world too huge to exist.

Nid oes acw. Dim ond fi yw yma
Fi
Heb dad na mam na chwiorydd na brawd,
A'r dechrau a'r diwedd yn cau amdanaf.

Pwy wyf i? Pwy wyf i?
Estyn fy mreichiau ac yno, rhwng eu dau fôn
Arswydo meddwl amdanaf fy hun,
A gofyn gwaelod pob gofyn:
Pwy yw hwn?
Sŵn y dŵr. Bracsaf iddo am ateb.
Dim ond y rhediad oer.

Trwy'r clais adref os oes adref.
Swmpo'r post iet er amau,
Ac O, cyn cyrraedd drws y cefn,
Sŵn adeiladu daear newydd a nefoedd newydd
Ar lawr y gegin oedd clocs mam i mi.

There is no there. Only I is here,
I,
Without father or mother, without brother or sisters,
And the beginning and the end closing around me.

Who am I? Who am I?
My arms reached out and there, between their two stumps,
Terrified to think about myself
And asking the basis of all asking:
Who is this?
A noise of water. I waded into it for an answer.
Nothing, only the cold flow downward.

Home—if there is home—through the stream,
In my doubt touching the gate post, the mass of it,
And Oh, before I reached the back door,
Sound of new earth and new heaven being built
On the kitchen floor, were my Mam's clogs to me.

CYMRU'N UN

Ynof mae Cymru'n un. Y modd nis gwn.
    Chwiliais drwy gyntedd maith fy mod, a chael
Deunydd cymdogaeth—o'r Hiraethog hwn
    A'i lengar liw; a thrwy'r un modd, heb ffael,
Coleddodd fi ryw hen fugeiliaid gynt
    Cyn mynd yn dwr dros war y Mynydd Du,
A thrinwyr daear Dyfed. Uwch fy hynt
    Deffrowr pob cyfran fy Mhreseli cu.
A gall mai dyna pam yr wyf am fod
    Ymhlith y rhai sydd am wneud Cymru'n bur
I'r enw nad oes mo'i rannu; am ddryllio'r rhod
    Anghenedl sydd yn gwatwar dawn eu gwŷr;
Am roi i'r ysig rwydd-deb trefn eu tras.
Gobaith fo'n meistr: rhoed Amser inni'n was.

120

WALES ONE

In me is Wales one. How, I do not know.
    All the fore-courts of my being I've searched, and found
The stuff of neighbourhood. From Hiraethog, so
    Steeped in literature. Equally sound
I was nourished by the old shepherds, till they
    Crossed over Mynydd Du into the Valleys,
And by tillers of Dyfed earth. Above my way,
    Awakeners everywhere, the dear Preselis.
That's why, perhaps, I'm one of those who've sought
    To make Wales true to the undivided name,
And smash the anti-nation Juggernaut
    That mocks our people's talents; to give again
To the bruised the ease and order of their race.
    May hope be master, Time serve *us* a space.

CYMRU A CHYMRAEG

Dyma'r mynyddoedd. Ni fedr ond un iaith eu codi
A'u rhoi yn eu rhyddid yn erbyn wybren cân.
Ni threiddiodd ond un i oludoedd eu tlodi,
Trwy freuddwyd oesoedd, gweledigaethau munudau mân.
Pan ysgythro haul y creigiau drwy'r awyr denau,
Y rhai cryf uwch codwm, y rhai saff ar chwaraele siawns
Ni wn i sut y safant onid terfynau
Amser a'u daliodd yn nhro tragwyddoldeb dawns.
Tŷ teilwng i'w dehonglreg! Ni waeth a hapio
Mae'n rhaid inni hawlio'r preswyl heb holi'r pris.
Merch perygl yw hithau. Ei llwybr y mae'r gwynt yn chwipio,
Ei throed lle diffygiai, lle syrthiai, y rhai o'r awyr is.
Hyd yma hi welodd ei ffordd yn gliriach na phroffwydi.
Bydd hi mor ieuanc ag erioed, mor llawn direidi.

WELSH AND WALES

These mountains, only one language can lift them,
Give them their freedom, against a sky of song.
To the riches of their poverty only one pierced
Through a dream of ages, small moments of vision.
When, through thin air, sunlight etches the rocks
Strong over chasm, sure above playgrounds of chance—
How *do* they endure, unless the confines of time
Hold them in a turn, an eternity of dance?—
A home fit for her, their interpreter! No matter what,
We must claim this house, never asking the price.
And she is danger's daughter. Her path the wind whips,
Her feet where they tired, where they fell, those of the lower air.
Till now she has seen her way clearer than prophets.
She'll be as young as ever, as full of mischief.

YR HENIAITH

Disglair yw eu coronau yn llewych llysoedd
A thanynt hwythau. Ond nid harddach na hon
Sydd yn crwydro gan ymwrando â lleisiau
Ar ddisberod o'i gwrogaeth hen;
Ac sydd yn holi pa yfory a fydd,
Holi yng nghyrn y gorllewinwynt heno—
Udo gyddfau'r tyllau a'r ogofâu
Dros y rhai sy'n annheilwng o hon.

Ni sylwem arni. Hi oedd y goleuni, heb liw.
Ni sylwem arni, yr awyr a ddaliai'r arogl
I'n ffroenau. Dwfr ein genau, goleuni blas.
Ni chlywem ei breichiau am ei bro ddi-berygl
Ond mae tir ni ddring ehedydd yn ôl i'w nen,
Rhyw ddoe dihiraeth a'u gwahanodd.
Hyn yw gaeaf cenedl, y galon oer
Heb wybod colli ei phum llawenydd.

Na! dychwel gwanwyn i un a noddai
Ddeffrowyr cenhedloedd cyn eu haf.
Hael y tywalltai ei gwin iddynt.
Codent o'i byrddau dros bob hardd yn hyf.
Nyni, a wêl ei hurddas trwy niwl ei hadfyd,
Codwn, yma, yr hen feini annistryw.
Pwy yw'r rhain trwy'r cwmwl a'r haul yn hedfan,
Yn dyfod fel colomennod i'w ffenestri?

THE OLD LANGUAGE

Their crowns are radiant in the bright courts,
And they beneath them. But no lovelier than she
Who's a wanderer now, listening to voices
That have slipped their old fealty.
She asks herself what tomorrow there'll be,
Asks it in the teeth of the west wind—
In the throats of caves and crevices moaning
Over those unworthy of her.

We never noticed her. She was like light, she had no colour.
We never noticed. She was the air, took smell
To our nostrils. Was water on our lips, the light of taste.
We were not conscious of her arms round the land.
No danger then. Now, it's where larks
Do not climb back to heaven,
Some unwished yesterday has parted them.
This is a nation's winter—the cold heart
Does not know its five joys are lost.

No! spring will return to her, who fostered
Before their summer, wakeners of nations.
Generously she poured out her wine for them.
They rose from her tables bold for all beauty.
We that perceive her rank, through the mist of her troubles,
Let's raise here the old, indestructible stones.
Who are these flying through cloud and sun
Like doves to her windows?

Y GENI

Mor ddieithr, coeliaf i, fuasai i Fair
    A Joseff ein hanesion disglair ni
Am gôr angylion ac am seren, am dair
    Anrheg y doethion dan ei phelydr hi.
Ni bu ond geni dyn bach, a breintio'r byd
    I sefyll dan ei draed, a geni'r gwynt
Drachefn yn anadl iddo, a'r nos yn grud,
    A dydd yn gae i'w gampau a heol i'w hynt.
Dim mwy na phopeth deuddyn—onid oes
    I bryder sanctaidd ryw ymglywed siŵr,
A hwythau, heb ddyfalu am ffordd y groes,
    Yn rhag-amgyffred tosturiaethau'r Gŵr,
A'u cipio ysbaid i'r llawenydd glân
Tu hwnt i ardderchowgrwydd chwedl a chân.

NATIVITY

To Mary and Joseph, how unfamiliar would be
    The shining histories we tell tonight
Of a choir of angels and a star, and three
    Gifts of the Wise Men under its light!
It was but the birth of a child, a privileged world
    Beneath his feet, and the wind born again
As his breath. Night a cradle curled,
    And day a field to play in, road to gain.
Two people's everything, no more—unless
    To sacred care a sure propensity began
And they, not imagining the Cross, but blest
    By fore-feeling the compassions of the Man,
Snatched them a respite for pure joy, beyond
All the magnificence of fable and song.

WEDI'R CANRIFOEDD MUDAN

Wedi'r canrifoedd mudan clymaf eu clod.
Un yw craidd cred a gwych adnabod
Eneidiau yn un â'r rhuddin yng ngwreiddyn Bod.

Maent yn un â'r goleuni. Maent uwch fy mhen
Lle'r ymgasgl, trwy'r ehangder, hedd. Pan noso'r wybren
Mae pob un yn rhwyll i'm llygad yn y llen.

John Roberts, Trawsfynydd. Offeiriad oedd ef i'r tlawd,
Yn y pla trwm yn rhannu bara'r unrhawd,
Gan wybod dyfod gallu'r gwyll i ddryllio'i gnawd.

John Owen y Saer, a guddiodd lawer gwas,
Diflin ei law dros yr hen gymdeithas,
Rhag datod y pleth, rhag tynnu distiau'r plas.

Rhisiart Gwyn. Gwenodd am y peth yn eu hwyneb hwy:
'Mae gennyf chwe cheiniog tuag at eich dirwy',
Yn achos ei Feistr ni phrisiodd ef ei hoedl yn fwy.

Y rhedegwyr ysgafn, na allwn eu cyfrif oll,
Yn ymgasglu'n fintai uwchlaw difancoll,
Diau nad oes a chwâl y rhai a dalodd yr un doll.

Y talu tawel, terfynol. Rhoi byd am fyd,
Rhoi'r artaith eithaf am arweiniad yr Ysbryd,
Rhoi blodeuyn am wreiddyn a rhoi gronyn i'w grud.

Y diberfeddu wedi'r glwyd artaith, a chyn
Yr ochenaid lle rhodded ysgol i'w henaid esgyn
I helaeth drannoeth Golgotha eu Harglwydd gwyn.

Mawr ac ardderchog fyddai y rhain yn eich chwedl,
Gymry, pe baech chwi'n genedl.

AFTER THE MUTE CENTURIES
(the Catholic martyrs)

I knot their praises, for long centuries mute.
The core of all faith is one, it is splendid to meet
With souls one with the quick at Being's root.

Over my head they are there, they are one with the light
Where through the expanse peace gathers. When night
Veils the sky, each is a shining gap in my sight.

John Roberts of Trawsfynydd, priest to the needy,
In the dread plague shared out the bread of the journey,
Knowing the powers of the dark had come, and would break his body.

John Owen the joiner, that many a servant concealed,
For the old communion his hand an unvarying shield,
Lest the plait be unravelled, and the beams of the great house yield.

Richard Gwyn smiled in their face at what they were at:
"I have sixpence towards your fine"—for he'd not
In the cause of his Master, price his life more than that.

They that ran light, I cannot number them all,
A company gathered together beyond the pits of hell:
Surely nothing can scatter them who paid the self-same toll.

The last, quiet payment. World for world giving then,
For the Spirit to guide them giving that ultimate pain,
Giving a flower for the root, for his cradle a grain.

Torture did rack them, disembowelling rend,
Ere the sight where a ladder was given their souls to ascend
To the broad next morning of Golgotha, their blest Lord's world
                                        without end.

Welshmen, were you a nation, great would be the glory
These would have in your story.

PA BETH YW DYN?

Beth yw byw? Cael neuadd fawr
Rhwng cyfyng furiau.
Beth yw adnabod? Cael un gwraidd
Dan y canghennau.

Beth yw credu? Gwarchod tref
Nes dyfod derbyn.
Beth yw maddau? Cael ffordd trwy'r drain
At ochr hen elyn.

Beth yw canu? Cael o'r creu
Ei hen athrylith.
Beth yw gweithio ond gwneud cân
O'r coed a'r gwenith?

Beth yw trefnu teyrnas? Crefft
Sydd eto'n cropian.
A'i harfogi? Rhoi'r cyllyll
Yn llaw'r baban.

Beth yw bod yn genedl? Dawn
Yn nwfn y galon.
Beth yw gwladgarwch? Cadw tŷ
Mewn cwmwl tystion.

Beth yw'r byd i'r nerthol mawr?
Cylch yn treiglo.
Beth yw'r byd i blant y llawr?
Crud yn siglo.

WHAT IS MAN?

To live, what is it? It's having
A great hall between cramped walls.
To know another, what's that? Having
The same root under the branches.

To believe, what is it? Guarding a town
Until acceptance comes.
Forgiveness, what's that? A way through thorns
To an old enemy's side.

Singing, what is it? The ancient
Genius of the creation.
What's work but making a song
Of the trees and the wheat?

To rule a kingdom, what's that? A craft
That is crawling still.
And to arm it? You put a knife
In a baby's hand.

Being a nation, what is it? A gift
In the depths of the heart.
Patriotism, what's that? Keeping house
In a cloud of witnesses.

What's the world to the strong?
Hoop a-rolling.
To the children of earth, what is it?
A cradle rocking.

MEWN DAU GAE

O ba le'r ymroliai'r môr goleuni
Oedd a'i waelod ar Weun Parc y Blawd a Parc y Blawd?
Ar ôl imi holi'n hir yn y tir tywyll,
O b'le deuai, yr un a fu erioed?
Neu pwy, pwy oedd y saethwr, yr eglurwr sydyn?
Bywiol heliwr y maes oedd rholiwr y môr.
Oddi fry uwch y chwibanwyr gloywbib, uwch callwib y cornicyllod,
Dygai i mi y llonyddwch mawr.

Rhoddai i mi'r cyffro lle nad oedd
Ond cyffro meddwl yr haul yn mydru'r tes,
Yr eithin aeddfed ar y cloddiau'n clecian,
Y brwyn lu yn breuddwydio'r wybren las.
Pwy sydd yn galw pan fo'r dychymyg yn dihuno?
Cyfod, cerdd, dawnsia, wele'r bydysawd.
Pwy sydd yn ymguddio ynghanol y geiriau?
Yr oedd hyn ar Weun Parc y Blawd a Parc y Blawd.

A phan fyddai'r cymylau mawr ffoadur a phererin
Yn goch gan heulwen hwyrol tymestl Tachwedd
Lawr yn yr ynn a'r masarn a rannai'r meysydd
Yr oedd cân y gwynt a dyfnder fel dyfnder distawrwydd.
Pwy sydd, ynghanol y rhwysg a'r rhemp?
Pwy sydd yn sefyll ac yn cynnwys?
Tyst pob tyst, cof pob cof, hoedl pob hoedl,
Tawel ostegwr helbul hunan.

Nes dyfod o'r hollfyd weithiau i'r tawelwch
Ac ar y ddau barc fe gerddai ei bobl,
A thrwyddynt, rhyngddynt, amdanynt ymdaenai
Awen yn codi o'r cudd, yn cydio'r cwbl,
Fel gyda ni'r ychydig pan fyddai'r cyrch picwerchi
Neu'r tynnu to deir draw ar y weun drom.
Mor agos at ein gilydd y deuem—
Yr oedd yr heliwr distaw yn bwrw ei rwyd amdanom.

IN TWO FIELDS

Where did the sea of light roll from
Onto Flower Meadow Field and Flower Field?
After I'd searched for long in the dark land,
The one that was always, whence did he come?
Who, oh who was the marksman, the sudden enlightener?
The roller of the sea was the field's living hunter.
From above bright-billed whistlers, prudent scurry of lapwings,
The great quiet he brought me

Excitement he gave me, where only
The sun's thought stirred to lyrics of warmth,
Crackle of gorse that was ripe on escarpments,
Hosting of rushes in their dream of blue sky.
When the imagination wakens, who calls
Rise up and walk, dance, look at the world?
Who is it hiding in the midst of the words
That were there on Flower Meadow Field and Flower Field?

And when the big clouds, the fugitive pilgrims,
Were red with the sunset of stormy November,
Down where the ashtrees and maples divided the fields,
The song of the wind was deep like deep silence.
Who, in the midst of the pomp, the super-abundance,
Stands there inviting, containing it all?
Each witness' witness, each memory's memory, life of each life,
Quiet calmer of the troubled self.

Till at last the whole world came into the stillness
And on the two fields his people walked,
And through, and between, and about them, goodwill widened
And rose out of hiding, to make us all one,
As when the few of us forayed with pitchforks
Or from heavy meadows lugged thatching of rush,
How close we came then, one to another—
The quiet hunter so cast his net round us.

O, trwy oesoedd y gwaed ar y gwellt a thrwy'r goleuni y galar
Pa chwiban nas clywai ond mynwes? O, pwy oedd?
Twyllwr pob traha, rhedwr pob trywydd,
Hai! y dihangwr o'r byddinoedd
Yn chwiban adnabod, adnabod nes bod adnabod.
Mawr oedd cydnaid calonnau wedi eu rhew rhyn.
Yr oedd rhyw ffynhonnau'n torri tua'r nefoedd
Ac yn syrthio'n ôl a'u dagrau fel dail pren.

Am hyn y myfyria'r dydd dan yr haul a'r cwmwl
A'r nos trwy'r celloedd i'w mawrfrig ymennydd.
Mor llonydd ydynt a hithau a'i hanadl
Dros Weun Parc y Blawd a Parc y Blawd heb ludd,
A'u gafael ar y gwrthrych, y perci llawn pobl.
Diau y daw'r dirháu, a pha awr yw hi
Y daw'r herwr, daw'r heliwr, daw'r hawliwr i'r bwlch,
Daw'r Brenin Alltud a'r brwyn yn hollti.

Ages of blood on the grass and the light of grief,
Who whistled through them? Who heard but the heart?
The cheater of pride and every trail's tracker,
Escaper from the armies, hey, there's his whistling—
Knowledge of us, knowledge, till at last we do know him!
Great was the leaping of hearts, after their ice age.
The fountains burst up towards heaven, till
Falling back, their tears were like leaves of a tree.

Day broods on all this beneath sun and cloud,
And Night through the cells of her wide-branching brain—
How quiet they are, and she breathing freely
Over Flower Meadow Field and Flower Field—
Keeps a grip on their object, a field full of folk.
Surely these things must come. What hour will it be
That the outlaw comes, the hunter, the claimant to the breach,
That the Exiled King cometh, and the rushes part in his way?

[DUW]

Ni saif a llunio arfaeth orffenedig
O'n cystudd ni. Atom y rhed, a rhoi
Cymorth ei law yn ddirgel gan ddirgelwch
Na ellir ei ddatgloi.

'*Paham yr Wyf yn Grynwr*'—1956)

[GOD]

He does not stand devising consummate design
From our affliction. Look, he runs to us, and
Secretly, with a secret may not be unlocked,
Gives the help of his hand.

'Why I am a Quaker'—1956

LEAVES OF A TREE

Poems first published in *Dail Pren* 1956

GENETH IFANC

Geneth ifanc oedd yr ysgerbwd carreg.
Bob tro o'r newydd mae hi'n fy nal.
Ganrif am bob blwydd o'm hoedran
I'w chynefin af yn ôl.

Rhai'n trigo mewn heddwch oedd ei phobl,
Yn prynu cymorth daear â'u dawn.
Myfyrio dirgelwch geni a phriodi a marw,
Cadw rhwymau teulu dyn.

Rhoesant hi'n gynnar yn ei chwrcwd oesol.
Deuddeg tro yn y Croeso Mai
Yna'r cydymaith tywyll a'i cafodd.
Ni bu ei llais yn y mynydd mwy.

Dyfnach yno oedd yr wybren eang
Glasach ei glas oherwydd hon.
Cadarnach y tŷ anweledig a diamser
Erddi hi ar y copâu hyn.

A YOUNG GIRL

The skeleton of stone was once a young girl.
Always she's done it, she holds me now—
I go back for every year of my age
A century, to the world she knew.

Hers were a people who lived in peace.
The bounty of earth was theirs to win,
Pondering secrets of birth, marriage and death,
Keeping the ties of the brotherhood of man.

Early, they pitted her down for ever.
Twelve times she welcomed in the May
And then the dark companion took her.
Her voice was in the mountain no more.

The wide expanse of the sky was deeper then,
Bluer the blue of it because of her.
Stronger the house invisible and timeless
For her sake, on the hilltops here.

OHERWYDD EIN DYFOD

Oherwydd ein dyfod i'r ystafell dawel,
Yn yr ogof ddiamser yr oedd,
A'n myned allan i fanfrig gwreiddiau
Ac i afalau perllannoedd;
A'n myned allan trwy'r wythïen dywyll
I oleuni yr aelwydydd
A mi'n dilyn y galon gynnes
Seren fy nos a rhin fy nydd.

A chusan yn dychwel hyd bob seren
Eigion yr archipelágo,
A dwyfron yn adnewyddu daear
A dwy fraich yn gysgod y fro;
Oherwydd ein dyfod i'r tŷ cadarn
A'i lonydd yn sail i lawenydd ein serch
A dyfod y byd i'r dyfnder dedwydd
O amgylch sŵn troed fy eurferch.

BECAUSE OF OUR COMING

Because of our coming into the quiet room,
In the timeless cavern,
And because of our going out
Into the network of roots
And into orchards of apples,

And because of our going out
Through the dark veins
Into the light of bright hearths
And me, because of my following
The warm heart,
My night star,
My secret of day . . .

And a kiss out to every star restoring
The deep ocean, the archipelago,
And two breasts making a new earth,
Two arms sheltering the country . . .

Because of our coming to the house built strong
With peace its foundation
For the joy of our love,

And the world itself coming
To the deep happiness
Within sound of the footfall
Of my gold girl.

ANGHARAD

Dros lawer y pryderai
Liw nos, a chydlawenhâi,
Synhwyro'r loes, uno â'r wledd,
Yn eigion calon coledd.
I'w phyrth deuai'r trafferthus
A gwyddai'r llesg ddôr ei llys.
Gŵn sgarlad Angharad oedd
Hyd ei thraed, o weithredoedd.

Dwyn helbulon y fron frau,
Trwy'i chyfnerth trechu ofnau.
Ar ei glin y bore glas
Rhôi ei diwrnod i'r Deyrnas,
A rhoi symledd ei heddiw
Yn win i'r Brenin a'r briw.
Ymorol am Ei olud,
Ailgreu â'i fawl ddilwgr fyd.
Chwaer haul a chwaer awelon,
Chwaer i'r dydd lle chwery'r don,
A chwaer i'r sêr pryderus
Gan arial gofal eu gwŷs.

Torri dig a chenfigen,
Iacháu â ffrwythau ei phren,
Lledu'n rhad y llydan rodd.
Heb ing a'i llawn ehangodd,
Hiraeth yn tystiolaethu
O'i wraidd dwfn yn y pridd du.
Rhoddai i Dduw o'r ddwy wedd,
Ing a hoen yn gynghanedd.
Rhôi i ni yn awyr Nêr
Offeiriadaeth ei phryder.

ANGHARAD

Many by night she worried
Over, or rejoiced when they did,
Felt the woe, joined in the feast—
Those her heart's ocean cherished.
To her porch all in trouble
And the feeble knew her hall.
Angharad's gown of scarlet,
Woven of deeds, reached her feet.

She bore the care of sufferers
And with shared strength, cast out fears.
On her knees in the grey dawn
Gave her day to the Kingdom,
Today's simplicity bringing
As wine to the wounded King.
By praising God, over again
To create a world unfallen.
Sister of sun, of the breezes,
Of the day where the wave plays,
Sister to the anxious stars
In the zeal of their musters.

Broke down anger and envy,
Healed with the fruits of her tree,
Broadened the wide gift freely.
Old anguish opened her heart—
A yearning that bore witness
To its deep root in the soil.
She gave to God twofold care,
Both woe and joy together.
To us gave, like the sky of God,
Her anxiety's priesthood.

GYFAILL, MI'TH GOFIAF

Gyfaill, mi'th gofiaf,
Dy ben heulwen haf
A glyn y gaeaf galon gywir.
Ym mhob dyn mab dau
Gwelit y golau
Ac yng nghraidd y gau angerdd y gwir.

Llawr hud lle rhodiem
A gwawr fel gwawr gem
Am a ddadleuem oedd dy lewych.
Anian eneiniog
Isel dywysog
Yn ein Tir na n-Óg. Yno tau'r nych.

Dy chwerthin, gwin gwydr
Palas y pelydr
Pan lenwit ti fydr. Pan lunit fyd
Hyder mawr dramâu
Gweld byw, gweld beiau,
Diogel faddau, dy gelfyddyd.

Rhin bardd trwy straen byd,
Treiddfa tua'r rhwyddfyd.
Ei dŵr a gyfyd wedi gofal,
Arffed i orffwys.
A chân a'i chynnwys
Hoen y Baradwys, hen wybr Idwal.

I REMEMBER YOU, FRIEND
i.m. Idwal Jones

I remember you, friend—
Your summer sunshine head
And vale of the winter
True of heart.
In each man, son of two,
You would see light—
At falsehood's core
The force of the true.

We walked magic ground—
Your brightness haloed with light
Like a gem round
What we debated.
Anointed nature,
A lowly prince
In our Tir na n-Óg.
Mute now is weakness.

A wineglass your laughter,
Palace of sunbeams
As you filled your verse,
As you formed a world—
Audacity of dramas
To see life, see faults,
Forgiveness granted—
The way of your art.

Through strain of the world
The poet's magic
Reaches to ease.
Tower lofts after care.
A lap to rest on
And a song contains it—
Vivacity of Paradise,
Old sky of Idwal.

TRI BARDD O SAIS A LLOEGR

I

Pen pencerdd serch trwy'r rhwyg sy'n rhoi
Calon a chalon am y glyn,
A'i Dduw'n gysgadur di ddeffroi,
Yn dduw na wêl na'i ddu na'i wyn.

Haf ar y rhos wrth gefn ei dŷ
A dim ni syfl, yr hir brynhawn.
A disgwyl beth, O, lonydd lu,
Banadl a bedw a chyrs a chawn?

A dyr y Tosturiaethau yn un
Â chôr yr Oesoedd ar Ei glyw
A throi'n orfoledd? . . . Beth yw dyn?
A ddeffry ef ym meddwl Duw?

II

Medi ar feysydd hen Caer Wynt
A'r hwyr yn gwynnu sofl yr haidd.
O, Loegr, pan êl dy her i'w hynt
Hyn wyt i'th Greawdr yn dy graidd.

Yma un Medi daeth dy gawr
Pum troedfedd, sicr ynghanol sen.
A gwanwyn oedd y dyddiad mawr
A bery byth yn nail ei bren.

Dyheai'r haul cyn mynd i'r cudd
A hidlai'r hwyr yr adliw rhos.
A dôl i harddwch oedd y dydd
A glyn gwneud enaid oedd y Nos.

THREE ENGLISH POETS AND ENGLAND

I

Supreme love poet through the vale
That severs heart from heart's delight,
Whose sleeping God wakes not at all,
A God seeing neither black nor white.

Behind his house, June on the moor
And nothing stirs all the long noon.
What is the quiet waiting for—
Reedbed and birch, the rush, the broom?

One with the choir of Ages, can
The Mercies upon His ear break
And turn to joy? And what is man?
In the mind of God is he to wake?

II

Harvesting barley by Winchester town,
Evening whitens stubble and lea.
England, when your vaunt is gone,
This to your Maker is what you'll be.

Here, one harvest, your giant came,
Five foot tall, sure amid mockery,
And the great days were a springtime
Will last for ever as leaves of his tree.

How yearned the sun upon its way
As evening shed its rosy light.
A meadow of beauty was the day,
A vale of soul-making the night.

III

Ynghwsg y mae'r gweirgloddiau mawr
Lle llusg hen afon Ouse trwy'r llaid,
Ac felly'r oeddynt yn yr awr
Y ciliodd ef fel hydd o'r haid.

Ond yn ei encil clywodd lef
Ei frodyr dan yr isel frad—
Y caethwas du ymhell o'i dref
A'r caethwas gwyn ym mryntni'r gad.

Ac o'r tawelwch, wrtho ei hun,
Heriodd â'i gerdd anwaraidd gôr,
A'i freuder dros frawdoliaeth dyn
Trwy ddirgel ffyrdd yr Arglwydd Iôr.

IV

Nid am dy fawrion, Loegr, ychwaith,
Rhoddaf fy niolch iti'n awr,
Am iti dorri'r hyfryd iaith
Â mi, yn fy mlynyddoedd mawr.

A'th adar cerdd a dail y coed
Yn canu o gylch fy Linda lon,
Cydganu â mi amdani hi
Yn dwyn y fraint o dan y fron

Megis pan gyfyd haul ar fryn
Ac estyn obry rodd ei wres
A rhoi ei baladr gloyw trwy'r glyn
A phuro'r tarth a pheri'r tes.

III

Asleep are the great meadows of hay
Where ancient Ouse drags through the mud,
And so they were upon the day
When like a stag, he fled the herd.

But from his refuge heard the cry
Of his brothers betrayed from far—
Black slaves under an alien sky,
White slaves in the squalor of war.

And in the silence, by his song,
By his weakness, alone he stood
And for man's brotherhood, challenged wrong
Through the mysterious ways of God.

IV

Not for your great ones, England, though,
I give you my thanks now—because
Of your exchange of pleasant speech
That with me in my great years was.

Your bird song and leaf of the wood
Sang round about my Linda blest,
Together sang of her with me
Who bore the privilege in my breast

As when the sun rises on a hill
And his gift of warmth reaches down
And sets his bright shaft through the vale
And clears the mist on shining ground.

EIRLYSIAU

Gwyn, gwyn
Yw'r gynnar dorf ar lawr y glyn.
O'r ddaear ddu y nef a'u myn.
Golau a'u pryn o'u gwely pridd
A rhed y gwanwyn yn ddi-glwy
O'u cyffro hwy uwch cae a ffridd.

Pur, pur,
Wynebau perl y cyntaf fflur.
Er eu gwyleidd-dra fel y dur
I odde' cur ar ruddiau cain,
I arwain cyn y tywydd braf
Ymdrech yr haf. Mae dewrach 'rhain?

Glân, glân,
Y gwynder cyntaf yw eu cân.
Pan elo'r rhannau ar wahân
Ail llawer tân fydd lliwiau'r tud.
Ond glendid glendid yma dardd
O enau'r Bardd sy'n llunio'r byd.

SNOWDROPS

White, white
The crowd's early down the vale.
Out of black earth, heaven calls them.
Light buys them from the bed of mould,
And the spring runs without taint
From their waking over pasture and field.

Strong, strong
The pearl faces of the earliest flower—
For all their modesty, like steel
To bear blows on the lovely cheeks
And lead out, before warm weather,
Summer's array. Are there braver than they?

Pure, pure
Is their song, the primal white.
When the shards of it scatter
Like a myriad fires they'll colour the fields.
But here it is purity, purity springs
From the Poet's lips who fashions the world.

HEB DEITL

Nid oes yng ngwreiddyn Bod un wywedigaeth
Yno mae'n rhuddin yn parhau.
Yno mae'r dewrder sy'n dynerwch
Bywyd pob bywyd brau.

Yno wedi'r ystorm y cilia'r galon.
Mae'r byd yn chwâl,
Ond yn yr isel gaer mae gwiwer gwynfyd
Heno yn gwneud ei gwâl.

UNTITLED

At the root of Being there's not one witheredness.
The heartwood is safe.
There the courage that is tenderness
Is life of every fragile life.

When the storm's over, there the heart flies.
All's scattered away,
But in the low fort the squirrel of bliss
Tonight makes its drey.

YR EILIAD

Nid oes sôn am yr Eiliad
Yn llyfr un ysgolhaig.
Peidia'r afon â rhedeg
A gwaedda'r graig
Ei bod hi'n dyst
I bethau ni welodd llygad
Ac ni chlywodd clust.

Awel rhwng yr awelon
Haul o'r tu hwnt i'r haul,
Rhyfeddodd y gwir gynefin
Heb dro, heb draul
Yn cipio'r llawr—
Gwyddom gan ddyfod yr Eiliad
Ein geni i'r Awr.

THE MOMENT

The Moment's mentioned
In no scholar's book.
River stops running,
Rock shouts, Look—
There's witness here
To things eyes do not see
Nor ears hear.

Breeze among breezes,
Sun from beyond the sun:
The marvel of that true home
Where wear and tear don't run
Steals the floor—
Because the Moment comes, we know
The Hour is what we're for.

YN NYDDIAU'R CESAR

Yn nyddiau'r Cesar a dwthwn cyfrif y deiliaid
    Canwyd awdl oedd yn dywyll i'w nerth naïf.
Ym Methlehem Effrata darganfu twr bugeiliaid
    Y gerddoriaeth fawr sy tu hwnt i'w reswm a'i rif.
Y rhai a adawai'r namyn un pump ugain
    Er mwyn y gyfrgoll ddiollwng—clir ar eu clyw
Daeth cynghanedd y dydd cyn dyfod y plygain
    Am eni bugail dynion, am eni Oen Duw.
Rai bychain, a'm cenedl fechan, oni ddyfalwch
    Y rhin o'ch mewn, nas dwg un Cesar i'w drefn?
Ac oni ddaw'r Cyrchwr atom ni i'r anialwch,
    Oni ddaw'r Casglwr sydd yn ein geni ni drachefn,
A'n huno o'n mewn yn gân uwchlaw Bethlehem dref?
Ein chwilio ni'n eiriau i'w awdl mae Pencerdd Nef.

IN THE DAYS OF CAESAR

There went out a decree that all
the world should be taxed
Luke, 2, 1

In the days of Caesar was an awdl sung,
    Was dark to the naivety of his might.
In Bethlehem Ephratah, to the shepherds rang
    The great music beyond his reckoning or right.
They were the folk who'd leave the ninety and nine
    For the one gone astray—clear to them, before dawn,
Came the cynghanedd and the answering rhyme
    Of the day Man's Shepherd and God's Lamb was born.
Little ones, and my little nation, can't you guess
    The secret within you no Caesar can tax?
Doesn't the Fetcher in the wastes come for us,
    The Gatherer we're born in again, bring us back,
Making us one within us, a song over Bethlehem town?
Words for his awdl we are, he searches, writes us down.

159

ENEIDFAWR

Eneidfawr, nid cawr ond cyfaill, a'i nerth yn ei wên yn dygyfor
O'r gwaelod lle nid oes gelyn, yn tynnu trwy ruddin ei wraidd.
Siriol wrth weision gorthrymder fel un a'i rhyddhâi o'u hualau
A throednoeth trwy'u cyfraith y cerddodd i ymofyn halen o'r môr.
Nid digon oedd teml ei dadau i atal ei rawd â'i pharwydydd,
I ganol y carthwyr ysgymun â'i ysgubell a'i raw yr aeth
Gan gredu, os un yw Duw, un ydyw dynion hefyd,
Gan droedio hen dir adnabod lle chwyth awelon y nef,
Gan wenu ar geidwad y carchar ac arwain ei genedl allan,
Ei dosturi ef a'i casglodd a'i ddewrder ydoedd y ddôr,
Gan ymbil eto â'r rhwygwyr, hyd fawrdro y cyfarch a'r cofio,
Cododd ei law ar ei lofrudd a myned trwy'r olaf mur.

GREAT-SOUL

Great-Soul, not giant but friend:
   his strength in a smile
Flooding up from depths
   where no enemies are, the pith of his root.
Cheerful with lackeys of tyranny
   as if he would free them from fetters,
Walking barefoot through their law
   to fetch salt from the sea.
The temple of his fathers
   with its castes could not stop him,
He went with his shovel and brush
   among the cursed sweepers,
Believed that if God is one,
   men are one also.
He walked an old land to acknowledge
   where the breezes of heaven blow.
He smiled at the prison warder
   as he led his nation out.
His pity was what gathered it,
   his courage was the door.
Still pleading with those who would tear it,
   turning, he greets, he remembers,
He lifts a hand to his killer—
   the last wall he goes through.

Y CI COCH

A glywsoch
Y stori am y ci coch,
Hwnnw a'i drwyn main a'i gain gwt
A'i ergyd tua'r ieirgwt?
'Fy haeddiant,' eb ef 'heddiw
Yw un hwyaden wen wiw
Cyn y daw Owen heno
I roi'r drws dan ei glws glo.'
Gyda'r hwyr o'i goed yr aeth
I ymyl caeau amaeth.
A daeth dan ddistaw duthian
A herc glir i barc y lan.
Yr oedd y fad hwyaden
Yn tolcio pridd ger twlc pren.
Heb Nos da, heb un ystŵr
Daeth y ffals, daeth y ffowlswr.
Cododd Gwen ei phen heb ffws
A fflip a fflap, hi fflopws
I'r twlc trwy'r siwter talcen
A chau'r drws bach. Chwerw dros ben!
A ba! dyna ei dinas.
Mae'n popo mewn, pipo ma's
A dweud, 'Cwac' a 'Dic dac do,
'Dwy' i ddim yn ffit it eto!'

THE RED DOG

Have you heard
The story of the red dog,
Him with the nose and fine brush
And designs on the henhutch?
'I deserve today,' says he,
'A white duck, nice and juicy,
Before that Owen comes, to lock
For the night, their pretty padlock.'
Twilight, from his wood he steals
To the edge of the plowfields
Trotting quiet and froward,
And hop! to the village yard.
There's luck! the good duck pecking
The ground near a wooden hut.
With never a good-night to her
The false one comes, the fowler.
Ah, but Gwen—no fuss—looks up
And flaps to the hutch, flipflop
Through the shutter, pushes her
And the door closes. O bitter!
But bingo! here's her hide-out.
She's popping in, peeping out,
Says, 'Quack,' and 'Dick-dack-do
I'm not yet yours to swallow!'

MEDI

Uchel yw pren y bydoedd
A Medi ydyw'r mis
Y plyg yr haul mawr aeddfed
Ei ystwyth gainc yn is.

A than ei thrymlwyth hithau
Mae cainc o'r pren sy'n hŷn
Yn gwyro trwy'r llonyddwch
I lawr at galon dyn.

A rhwng tymhorau daear
Ymrithia amgen wedd.
Ynghanol oesol ryfel
Mihangel y mae hedd.

HARVEST

The tree of the worlds is lofty
But in September now
The great ripe sun is bending
The branches of it low.

So too beneath its burden
A more ancient tree is fraught,
Inclining through the stillness
Down towards man's heart;

And between earth's seasons
Puts on a different face.
Amid the perpetual warfare
Of Michael, there is peace.

LATER POEMS

1960-70

1960   Llwyd [*Beirdd Penfro*, gol. W. Rhys Nicholas (1961), p.148-9]
1962   Cân imi, wynt [*Taliesin*, 3] Sing to me, Wind
1969   Gwenallt [*Cerddi '69*, gol. Gwilym Rees Jones ac Islwyn Jones, p. 71]
       Y Dderwen Gam [*Cerddi '69*, p. 71] The Crooked Oak
1970   Llandysilio-yn-Nyfed [*Cerddi '70*, gol. Bedwyr Lewis Jones, p. 79]

LLWYD

Mae'r holl iaith os marw yw Llwyd?
Nid yw brawddeg ond breuddwyd,
A'r niwl oer ar y waun lom
Os trengodd ystyr rhyngom.
Duw glân, Tad y goleuni,
Dyro'n ôl Dy wawr i ni.
Dy galon yw D'ogoniant,
'E dardd serch yn Dy wraidd sant.
Uwch ein clai Dy serch a'n clwm,
Iach y cydi uwch codwm.
Trig ynom trwy'r gwahanu
A thro ein taith i'r un Tŷ.

Oedd im frawd heb ddim o frith,
Addfwynder oedd ei fendith.
Llwyd, Nos da! Lledneisied oedd,
Goludog a gŵyl ydoedd.
Ynddo, nodd y winwydden
Yn ddilys ewyllys wen.
Eang a mwyn rhyngom oll,
Dygai'r cynhaeaf digoll.

Hir dymor yn Rhydaman,
Bugail oedd, a'i wyneb glân.
Gwas da am geisio deall,
Arwain Un i rin y llall,
I'r cyflawnder ni dderyw,
Hwsmonaeth cymdogaeth Duw.

Fy hiraethlef ar frithlawr,
Llwyd, cêl fardd Allt Cilau-fawr.
Golau a draidd i'w gwlad rith,
Aeth o'r haul ei hathrylith.
Ac oddi cartref hefyd
Aeth cu fab Wythcae o Fyd.

LLWYD

If Llwyd's dead, what's all language?
No sentence more than a dream,
A cold mist on a bare moor,
If meaning's lost between us.
Pure God, father of light, bring
Back to us your bright dawning.
Your glory is your heart. Love shoots
From you, up from the saint root.
Your love's tied above our clay,
Knots over fall a safe stay.
In our severance dwell, so we
Into one House may journey!

My brother, to me faultless,
His blessing was gentleness,
Llwyd, good night! O how meek was—
How rich, how modest he was!
And the sap of the vine still
Flowed in him, a sure goodwill.
Open and mild amongst us, unlost
He carried home the harvest.

Shepherd, with his honest face,
In Rhydaman a long space
(Good steward) tried to see sense,
Bring hearts into God's presence,
The unfailing fullness, God's
Husbandry of neighbourhood.

My cry of loss on flecked floor,
Llwyd, hid bard of Allt Cilau-fawr.
On phantoms light has broken,
Its genius has left the sun.
And from his home and threshold
The dear man left Wythcae's world—

169

Rhoes heibio droedio ei drum
Er dwylath yn Rhydwilym.
Och mae creu dychymyg rhydd?
Mawr wân yw marw awenydd.
Cod ein tras, cadw ein trysor,
Cwn dy lwyth i'n cenedl, Iôr.
A'r tarth a roet wrth y rhyd
Tro'n haul i'r tair anwylyd.

Mad enaid, gad im d'annerch.
Daw'r golau'n hardd drwy'r glyn erch.
Caf dy falm mewn cof di-feth,
Cyfyd brig haf dy bregeth
I ganu byth 'Gwyn eu byd
Y rhai addfwyn'. Ireiddfyd
Pregeth loyw, pur gathl eos.
Llawn o Nef yw llwyn y nos.
Ynddi mae d'awen heno.
Tywynna'r fraint, taena'r fro.

Gave up walking the hill brim
For two yards in Rhydwilym.
Oh, where's vision, free created?
A great wound is a poet's death.
Raise our race, keep our folk hoard,
Lift your burden on us, Lord,
And for the three dear ones, turn
Mist at the ford to sunshine.

Let me greet you, good soul. Glinted
Light breaks through the vale of dread.
I keep your balm for always,
Preaching, that tips summer days
To sing for ever, 'Blessed
Are the meek.' A glitter, a glad
Preaching, a nightingale's tune—
The grove of night's full of heaven.
Your music is there. Shine, and
Spread its gift over the land.

CÂN IMI, WYNT

Cân imi, wynt, o'r dyfnder ac o'r dechrau.
Cân imi, y dychymyg mwyaf maes.
Harddach na golau haul dy gerddi tywyll,
Y bardd tu hwnt i'n gaeaf ym mhob oes.

Fe genit imi'n grwt yn Ysgol Arberth
A llamu'n uwch na'm llofft o Ros y Dref,
Fy nghuddio â'th gyfrinach heb ei rhoddi,
A minnau ynddi ac amdani'n glaf.

Mi lanwaf y dirgelwch â'm blynyddoedd,
Cans dan y bargod canu'r oet, mi wn,
Am bethau oedd i fod nes myned ymaith
Ac aros hefyd yn y galon hon.

Cân imi, wynt: nid wyf yn deall eto
Y modd y rhoi i'n tristwch esmwythâd;
Cân inni, enau'r harddwch anorchfygol.
Ti wyddost am y pethau sydd i fod.

SING TO ME, WIND

Sing to me, wind, from the deeps, from the beginning,
Sing, imagination greatest of all,
Your dark songs lovelier than sunlight,
Poet, in every age, beyond what we know.

You sang to me as a schoolboy at Arberth,
Strode from Rhos y Dref above my loft,
Hid me with fellowship—not that you gave it—
I was in it, though, and yearning for it.

I fulfil the mystery with my years
For under the eaves you were singing, I know,
What things were to be, till you went your way
And also what in this heart would stay.

Sing to me, wind. I don't understand yet
The way you give our sadness ease.
Mouth of invincible beauty, sing to me.
You know of the things that are to be.

GWENALLT

Crych fu ei ganu; yn y gwaelod, crwn;
  Bethesda a gynhyrfid i'n hiacháu.
Ym mhoethni'r brwydro dros ein tegwch twn,
  Amynedd y gelfyddyd sy'n boddhau.
Harddwch arswydus 'purwr iaith ei lwyth,'
  Rhoes angerdd dan ei bron a nerth i'w braich
A gosod difrod yn y meddwl mwyth.
  Gwrolodd y Gymraeg i godi ei baich.
Nid rhyfedd hyn. Cafodd yr ennyd awr
  Nad oes mo'i dirnad, a'r dychymyg drud
A wêl yn hen wrthebau plant y llawr
  Y Breichiau praff yn crynu o dan y byd
Gan bryder santaidd; a'i ddyheu a roes
  I Frenin Nef yn marw ar y Groes.

GWENALLT

His song was wrinkled, but at bottom, round.
It was Bethesda, stirred to heal our hurt.
Even in hot battle over our beauty's wound,
What pleases is the patience of the art.
He 'purified the language of his tribe',
Which 'terrible beauty' put passion in her breast
And devastation in her indolent thought.
To lift her load, he gave Welsh heart and zest.
Nor is this strange. He had an hour's space,
One incomprehensible hour, and insight to see
In the old paradoxes of our race
The strong Arms trembling in holy anxiety
Under the world; and gave his gasping breath
To the King of Heaven dying on the Cross.

Y DDERWEN GAM
(Pan fwriedid cau ar ran uchaf Aberdaugleddau)

Rhedodd y môr i fyny'r afon
　　Y cyrliog serchog, pur ei drem
Unwaith, a myrdd o weithiau wedyn
　　Cyn imi gael y dderwen gam.

Cyn imi ddod yr hydref hwnnw
　　A sefyll dan y gainc a'u gweld,
Hithau a'i mynwes yn ymchwyddo'n
　　Ardderchog rhwng ei gwyrdd a'i gold.

Yma bydd llyn, yma bydd llonydd,
　　Oddi yma draw bydd wyneb drych;
Derfydd ymryson eu direidi
　　Taw eu tafodau dan y cwch.

Derfydd y llaid, cynefin chwibanwyr
　　Yn taro'r gerdd pan anturio'r gwawl,
A'u galw gloywlyfn a'u horohïan,
　　A'u llanw yn codi bad yr haul.

Yn codi'r haul ac yn tynnu'r eigion
　　Trwy'r calonnau gwyrdd dros y ddwylan lom,
Yma bydd llyn, yma bydd llonydd
　　A'r gwynt ym mrig y dderwen gam.

THE CROOKED OAK
(when it was planned to dam the upper part
of Aberdaugleddau)

The sea ran up into the river,
   The curling lovely, the pure of look,
Once, and a myriad times thereafter
   Before I found the crooked oak.

Before I came in that October,
   Stood under it, saw the branches wild,
The river with its bosom surging
   Splendid between the green and gold.

There'll be lake here, there'll be quiet,
   Stretching away a mirroring sheet,
An end of mischief and contention—
   Tongues are dumb below a boat.

The mire is finished, the haunt of whistlers—
   When the light ventures, strike up song.
The bright calls fluent, passionate, joyful,
   Their floodtide lifts the boat of the sun.

They lift the sunrise, pull the ocean
   To the green heart between bare banks.
There'll be a lake here, there'll be quiet,
   And wind in the tips of the crooked oak.

LLANDYSILIO-YN-NYFED

Mynych rwy'n syn. Pa olau o'r tu hwnt
   Eglurodd Grist i'w etholedig rai
Pan oedd ein byw yn farus ac yn frwnt
   Heb fawr o'i fryd na'i ddelfryd ar ein clai?
Rwy'n cofio fel yr aem i ddrws y tŷ
   Pan ganai cloch y llan am flwyddyn well;
Roedd mwynder Maldwyn eto ar Ddyfed gu
   Pan âi'r dychymyg ar ei deithiau pell
Yn nhrymder nos. Gwelem y fintai fach
   Heb ddinas camp yn ieuo'r byd yn un.
Ac yn eu plith gwelem yn glaerwyn iach
   Yn wenfflam gan orfoledd Mab y Dyn
Dysilio alltud na chwenychai'i sedd
   Ym Meifod gynt, rhag gorfod tynnu cledd.

LLANDYSILIO-YN-NYFED

I am often amazed. What light came from beyond
  That to his elect ones Christ could reveal
When life for us was brutal, full of wrong,
  Made great by neither purpose nor ideal?
I remember how we'd all go to the door
  When the church bell rang for a better year—
Maldwyn's gentleness on Dyfed once more
  As the imagination far and near
Travelled deep night. We'd see small companies,
  Without exploit of cities, yoke the world one
And among them, salvation clear, we'd see
  In the white flame rejoicing for God's son
Tysilio, who rather than draw his sword
  Chose exile here, ceased to be Meifod's lord.

A P P E N D I X

Tŷ Ddewi—St David's

The *Awdl* (1936, revised 1956)
with a translation by Dafydd Johnston
and notes by T.C.

TŶ DDEWI

Nos Duw am Ynys Dewi.
Daw hiraeth llesg i draeth lli.
Llif ar ôl llif yn llefain
Ymysg cadernid y main.
Araith y cof yw hiraeth y cyfan,
Hiraeth am y fro ar y gro a'r graean.
Mae hun fawr ym Mhen y Fan—a thrwyddi
Mae hiraeth am weilgi ym Mhorth Maelgan.

Yn weddus a gosgeiddig
Daw i'w draeth o dŷ ei drig.
Araf ei sang, i'w dangnef
O'i uchel waith dychwel ef.
Erddo'ch dywennydd rhoddwch, O donnau,
Yn gôr digyrrith a byddwch chwithau
Yn deilwng o'i sandalau, dywod mân,
Ymysg y graean cymysg o grïau.

O'i ofal daw fel y daeth
I dywod ei feudwyaeth,
Y gŵr tal a garai ton
A chlegyr uwchlaw eigion.
A'r tonnau taer, ar y tywyn torrant,
A'u lleisiau is, eilwaith, lle sisialant.
'Dewi ydyw' dywedant—a mwyned
Eu min agored am enw a garant.

Neu i'r gwron her gawraidd,
Tyred, wynt, a rhed â'i aidd
Uwchlaw'r gwanegau achlân
Gan chwythu'r gwŷn uwch weithian.
A chwithau'r un fel y tonnau melyn
Ymhyrddiwch a chorddwch dan lech Hwrddyn
A mawr dwrf rhag camre dyn o afiaith
A rhyddid hirfaith moroedd y terfyn.

ST DAVID'S

God's night over David's Island.
A faint yearning comes to the sea strand.
Flood after flood calls out
amidst the stones' solidity.
Memory's speech is all the yearning,
yearning for the land on the gravel and sand.
There is a long sleep in Pen y Fan, and through it
there is yearning for the ocean in Porth Maelgan.

Graceful and elegantly
he comes to his beach from the house where he dwells.
With measured pace he returns
from his exalted work to his peace.
For his sake give your happiness, O waves,
like a bountiful choir, and be you
worthy of his sandals, fine sand,
amongst the pebbles and strips of seaweed.

He comes from his charge as he came
to the sand of his hermit's life,
the tall man beloved by wave
and cliff above the ocean.
And the fervent waves break on the dunes,
and their voices whisper below once more.
'It is David' they say, and their lips are so tender
about the name which they love.

Or come, wind, in colossal challenge
to the hero, and run with his zeal
above all the waves
blowing the foam up higher now.
And you likewise, the yellow waves,
crash and foam beneath Hwrddyn's rock
with great tumult before the path of a man of zeal
and the vast freedom of the seas.

Mae eigion golygon glas
Ac o'u mewn y gymwynas.
Dewrder o dan dynerwch
Duw ni ludd i'r dynol lwch.
A glain y ddau oedd dy galon, Ddewi;
Trwy storom enaid rhoist dy rym inni,
A thrwy'r storom heb siomi yr hedd rhwydd,
Hafan distawrwydd y dwfn dosturi.

Nos Duw am Ynys Dewi.
Yntau, llaes yng ngwynt y lli
Ei glog, a'r grog ar arw grys
Yn rhyw ogian o'i wregys.
Draw'r oedd Hwrddyn ag ewyn yn gawod,
I'w hochr y glynai, a chri gwylanod.
Âi Dewi ar ei dywod. Yn y sŵn
Hyn a fu fyrdwn ei hen fyfyrdod:

Gado cysur seguryd
A dôr balch gwychterau byd
Am drech dawn yr ymdrech deg
Na chwennych ddawn ychwaneg.
Gado'r hen air a gado'r anwiredd
Gyda'r hen fâr gado'r hen oferedd.
Gado'r clod o godi'r cledd mewn byd claf
A thyngu i Naf waith a thangnefedd.

Gado, uwch mwynder ceraint,
Rhyddid serch am freuddwyd saint,
Am ddawn offrymu i Dduw
Rym enaid ar dir Mynyw,
Am lwm gilfeydd ac am lem gelfyddyd
Er gwaith ei wylltir i'w gaeth a'i alltud—
Rhwygo'r cryfder yn weryd—a throi a hau
Braenar y bau i Brynwr y Bywyd.

There is an ocean of blue visages
and within them is kindness.
Bravery beneath tenderness
is not denied mankind by God.
And your heart, David, was the jewel of both;
through the soul's storm you gave us your strength,
and through the storm unstinting the easy peace,
deep pity's haven of silence.

God's night over David's Island.
He stood with cloak hanging loose
in the sea-wind, and the cross on his rough shirt
swinging from his belt.
Hwrddyn was nearby, drenched in foam
which clung to its side, and the cry of seagulls.
Dewi walked on his sand. In the tumult
this was the burden of his old meditation:

To leave the comfort of idleness
and the proud door of worldly splendours
for the greater gift of the good fight
which desired no further reward.
Leave the old word and leave falsehood
and with the old anger leave the old vanity.
Leave the fame of raising the sword in a sick world
and dedicate work and peace to the Lord.

Leave, above kin's tenderness,
the freedom of love for the saints' dream,
for the honour of offering to God
a soul's strength on Menevia's land,
for bare retreats and for harsh craft
to work the wasteland for serf and foreigner—
tearing the hardness into fruitful soil and turning and sowing
the fallow land for the Redeemer of Life.

E dyr hwrdd yr aradr hon
Lawr brith y Gael a'r Brython.
Gras y Tywysog a red
Yn rhydd ofer o Ddyfed.
Daw bore Iesu o'i oriau duon
A siantau taer y llu seintiau tirion.
Ymlid braw o deimlad bron fydd Ei rad.
Daw dyn i'w gariad o dan Ei goron.

Ei gof o'r môr a gyfyd
Golch Ei fawl o gylch Ei fyd.
Cyfle saint a braint eu bro—
Tân Melita'n aml eto.
Y meithder, gan y sêr a fesurir,
Y lle ni phwyntiodd na llyw na phentir
Gan feudwy a dramwyir yn ddidrist
A bydd crog Crist lle bydd cerrig rhostir.

Iwerddon, parth â hwyrddydd,
A'r Iôr ar Ei fôr a fydd,
Glyned rhôm a'n glaniad draw.
Ymleda'r glas am Lydaw—
Tir y meudwyaid yw'r trumiau duon,
O'r conglau twn y daw'r cenglau tynion.
Yma bydd cof am Samson ein brodyr.
A hardd yr egyr hen ffyrdd yr eigion.

Hawddamor pan angoro
Mynaich, a thros fraich y fro
Pysgotwyr ar antur ŷnt,
Eneidiau cadarn ydynt.
Dan Glomen Wen, dan glymu'n ewynnau
Fawl a thrafael dyfalwaith y rhwyfau
Cipiant o galon y tonnau byddar
Hir wobrwy daear yr Hebredeau.

The thrust of this plough will break
the mottled ground of Gael and Briton.
The Prince's grace will run
in flowing streams from Dyfed.
Jesus's morning will come from His hours of darkness
and the fervent chants of the saintly host.
His blessing will expel terror from the heart.
People will come to His love beneath His crown.

His memory will rise from the sea,
His praise will wash around His world.
Saints' domain and the honour of their country—
Melita's fire will be frequent again.
The vastness, which is measured by the stars,
the place which was never eyed by lord or steward
will be joyfully traversed by a hermit
and Christ's cross will stand amongst moorland stones.

Ireland, towards evening,
and the Lord will be on His sea,
may He stand firm between us and our landing yonder.
The blue spreads out towards Britanny—
the dark ridges are the land of the hermits,
the tight girths come from the rugged corners.
Here Samson of our brothers will be remembered.
And the old ways of the ocean open beautifully.

Welcome when monks cast anchor,
and over the country's ridge
they are fisherman venturing their nets,
they are strong souls.
Under holy Columba, turning
praise and hard toil of the oars into knots of foam
they pluck from the heart of the deaf waves
the long reward of the land of the Hebrides.

Terfynwyd y proffwydo
Gan hir grych yn rhygnu'r gro.
A Dewi'n gweld trwy'r düwch
Ryw ŵr, pysgotwr o'i gwch
Oedd a'i gyfarchiad cynnes wrth nesu
Yn esgud wŷs i ddysgu Duw Iesu,
Mae Dewi'n sôn am y dawn sy i'r byd,
Am Un a'i gweryd ym mhoen ei garu.

Ni fynnai'r llall mo'i allu.
Ai rhan Duw oedd y drain du?
Dywawd, 'Nid af yn daeog
I Grist yn hongian ar grog.
Dyro'n ôl haul yr henfyd goleulon,
Dyre â golau i dir y galon
Heb un cur o boen coron gwrthuni
O, dyro inni adar Rhiannon'.

Ebr Dewi 'Cân y fanon
Fydd hoyw yn y grefydd hon;
Yn y newydd ffydd ni phaid
Hen degwch Brân Fendigaid.
Hwnnw oedd gyfiawn yn ei ddigofaint
A rhoddodd i'w dorf rad ei ragorfraint
Bu'n bont ar lawr, ei fawr faint. Bu'n heol
A dawn i ddwyfol, dwyn ei oddefaint.

'A chadarn a gwych ydoedd.
I osgo Duw cysgod oedd.
Eilun hil yn ehelaeth
Rithio Nef, ond syrthio wnaeth.
Ni ddaeth ef adref yn ei wrhydri
A'i hen gerdd arwest a gwŷr y ddyri.
Yn ei dranc bu fwyn dy ri. O'i galon
Adar Rhiannon roes i drueni.

The prophesying was brought to an end
by a long ripple grating on the gravel.
Through the darkness David saw a man,
a fisherman who greeted him warmly
from his boat as he approached
in urgent haste to learn of the Lord Jesus,
and David speaks of the gift to the world,
of One who will save it by the pain of loving it.

The other would have none of it.
Were the black thorns God's part?
He said, 'I will not serve
Christ hanging on a cross.
Give back the sun of the old shining world,
bring light to the land of the heart
without any pang of pain from an odious crown,
O, give us the birds of Rhiannon.'

'The song of that queen,' said David,
will still live in this religion;
the old beauty of Brân the Blessed
will not be lost in the new faith.
In his rage he was just
and with his own high privilege he graced his people,
laying his great length down as a bridge. He was a path
and medium for the divine through his suffering.

'And he was strong and splendid.
He foreshadowed God's shape.
A race's idol projected
a vast image of Heaven, but he fell.
he did not come home in his valour
with his old minstrelsy and men of song.
Your lord was kind in his death. From his heart
he gave the birds of Rhiannon as comfort.

'Eithr fe gyfodes Iesu
O'r llwch a'i dywyllwch du.
Yno nid erys unawr.
Engyl Ei efengyl fawr
Yw'r seren fore sy â'i rhin firain
A'r haul a dyr o hualau dwyrain,
Duw pob dydd a rydd trwy'r rhain Ei ienctid,
Penlinia o'i blegid pan leinw blygain.

'Eiddo i Nêr byddwn ni
A glân fel y goleuni
O law Nêr, goleuni iach
Bore syml, ba ras amlach?
Pob pen bore mae eilwyrth y Crëwr
Eiliad o'i hangerdd rhag golud ungwr.
Na, bord wen a bara a dŵr fo dy raid,
A gwêl dy lygaid y gwawl dilwgwr.'

Yna'n deg daeth blaen y dydd
I ymylon y moelydd.
Ond Dewi ni phenliniodd.
Llyma'r wawd a'r llam a rodd:
'Hyfryd oleuni a'i afradlonedd
Llamaf ar oror fy ngwlad lle gorwedd
Agored i'w drugaredd, a'r nos fawr—
Chwâl ar un awr a chilia'r anwiredd.'

II

Dyma hanfod Mehefin,
Lonydd haf trwy lonydd hin.
Ni ŵyr dail llwyn na brwyn bro
Hynt y nawn. Maent yn huno
Uwch erwau diog a chawr y deau
Yn rhoi ei danbeidrwydd rhwydd ar ruddiau
A chryndod mân gryndodau ei nerth tawdd
Yn firagl hawdd ar fieri'i gloddiau.

'But Jesus rose
from the dust and its black darkness.
He does not linger there a single hour.
The morning star that has such lovely power
is the angel of His great gospel
the sun which breaks out from the fetters of the east.
Through these every day God gives His youth,
kneel for His sake when He fills the dawn.

'We will belong to the Lord
and be pure as the light
from the Lord's hand, the healthy light
of a simple morning, what commoner grace?
At every break of day the Creator's miracle is repeated,
a second of its passion outweighs any man's wealth.
No, make do with a white table, bread and water,
and your eyes will see the uncorrupted light.'

At that very moment day's first light
came to the edges of the hills
but David did not kneel.
This was his song as he leapt to his feet:
'Lovely light and its plenitude,
I leap on the shore where my land
lies open to its mercy, and the great night—
it will scatter at once and falsehood will flee.'

II

Here is June's summer pasture,
the paths of summer through serene weather.
The leaves of the grove and the reeds of the land
know nothing of the afternoon. They are slumbering
over lazy acres whilst the giant of the south
pours his blazing heat over cheeks
and the trembling movement of his melting force
is an easy miracle on the briars of his hedges.

Pwy yw hi? Ymegnïa.
Serch ei hoed ar droed yr â.
Ai maith y daith y daethost?
Dyre, tynn 'am y droed dost
Yr esgid garpiog a rho dy glogyn
Hyd yma ar led am ryw eiliedyn.
Cei di hoe, cei wedi hyn ysbryd da
I fynd â'th yrfa'n fwyn hyd ei therfyn.

Dyre mor bell â Dowrog
Yno, clyw, cei daenu clog.
Mae rhos lle gwylia drosom
Y glas rhith sy'n eglwys rhôm.
A maith ei hallor a gwyrdd ei lloriau
Ac yno aderyn a gân dy oriau.
Yno os gwn cei ddi-lesgáu. Deui'n gynt
Heb reidus hynt, i baradwys seintiau.

Yn y frodir mae'r frawdiaith
A'th dyn yn 'sgafnach na'th daith.
Er dy fwyn, fe gredaf i,
Daw'r lleianod o'r llwyni.
Er mwyn 'r hen Fadlen yn ei thrueni . . .
Aros ni allet. O'r gwres enilli
Dy ddwywaith i Dŷ Ddewi cyn y floedd
Ar dy ingoedd yr awr y dihengi.

Ond wele ar yr heol
Eirian daith dros fryn a dôl,
Feirch agwrdd y farchogaeth
Gwaladr yw hyd Newgwl draeth.
Â gwayw ei henwlad a'i wŷr i'w ganlyn
I'w pader yn armaeth Pedr y Normyn
Er cyff Rhys, er coffa'r Rhosyn—yno,
A Duw a'u dalio wrth wlad y delyn.

Who is she? She makes haste.
Despite her age she goes on foot.
Was your journey long?
Come, take the ragged shoe
from your sore foot and spread out
your cloak here for a moment.
You can have a rest, and then you will be refreshed
to pursue your pleasant journey to its end.

Come as far as Dowrog,
listen, there you can spread your cloak.
There is a plain where we are guarded
by the green vision which is a church amongst us.
Vast is its altar and verdant its floors
and a bird there will sing your orisons.
There you can surely rest. You will come the sooner
without hardships to the saints' paradise.

In that land is the brotherly language
which will draw you more gently than your journey.
For your sake, I believe,
the nuns will come from the groves.
For the sake of old Magdalene in her wretchedness . . .
You could not wait. From the heat you will achieve
your two journeys to St David's before your agony's
death-cry in the hour you reach haven.

But behold on the road
a radiant journey over hill and dale,
mighty horses of knighthood.
It is a lord along Newgale beach.
With the spear of his old country and his band of men
going to pray in the service of Peter the Norman
for Rhys's stock, to commemorate the Rose there,
and may God keep them in the land of the harp.

Ac yma daw torf lawen
A chainc o'r ifainc a'r hen.
A phrins ymadroddi ffraeth
Yn neuadd i'r gwmnïaeth.
Ac yntau, ym mintai y palffreiod,
Y cawr gwenieithus, y câr genethod
Wrando ar ei bererindod ddiloes.
'Roedd hynny'n foes yn eu henoes hynod.

Eofn rhwng y colofnau
Yw'r llu mawr a'r holl ymwáu
Diatal. Ar wal, wele
Uwch llon ddigrifwch y lle,
Lu o nofisiaid dan law hen fasiwn.
Yntau a ddywed 'Mae'r gred a gredwn?
O mor hyll y miri hwn rhwng pethau
A riniodd wefusau'r hen ddefosiwn.

'Mae ofer sang yn nhangnef
Iesu Grist a'i gysegr Ef,
A lle mae yr hyll ymhél
Dewi a rodiai'n dawel.
O, am enaid hen ysbaid annisbur
Y saint meudwyol a wybu ddolur.
Hynt eu cân yr aethant, o'u cur. Dduw gwyn,
Y rhwydd ymofyn, lle'r oedd eu myfyr.

'Na wawdiwn gyffes Iesu,
Ysol dân yw sêl Ei dŷ.
Hir yma yr ymrwymais
A nwyd gwell i wneud Ei gais.
A muriau heddwch fydd am fy mreuddwyd
Yn nirgel lan y llan a ragluniwyd.
Hyd aml gôr y deml a gwyd o'm deutu
I'm hannwyl Iesu, y maen a lyswyd.

And here comes a merry band
with a song from young and old,
and a prince of witty speech
is a hall for the companionship.
And he, in the troop of palfreys,
the flattering giant, maidens love
to hear of his gentle pilgrimage.
That was the custom in those fine old times.

The great host goes boldly
between the columns and mingles
freely. Lo, on a wall
above the cheerful hubbub of the place,
a crew of novices led by an old mason.
Says he, 'Where's the faith we once held?
How repugnant is this merriment amongst things
which sanctified the lips of the old devotion.

'There is a vain throng in Christ's
peace and His sanctuary,
and an ugly swarm
where David once walked quietly.
O for the soul of the pure old age
of the solitary saints who knew suffering.
They have left their pain and followed their song. Holy God,
blatant self-seeking, where they once meditated.

'Let us not mock Christ's faith,
the zeal of His house is a consuming fire.
I have long been engaged here
to devote my energy to do His will.
And walls of peace will surround my dream
preordained in the church's hidden sanctuary.
Along many choirs the temple rises up around me
to my dear Jesus, the stone which was set at nought.

'Sibrydai mad Ysbryd mwyn
Ei Air i Fair y Forwyn.
Yn Ei wawl oni weli
Dlysineb Ei hwyneb Hi?
Erddi chwiliaf yr harddwch a welid
Ac uchel geinder fo'n gochel gwendid
Caf londer tra caf lendid—yn fy marn
Ar gerrig y darn a'r gwir gadernid.

'Fy Mair gu, y fam wâr gynt,
Annwyl pob un ohonynt.
Ond y Gair fu yn Dy gôl
A gerit yn rhagorol.
Un dymuniad a aned i minnau,
I ddal yr aing oni ddêl yr angau.
A naddu rhes fy nyddiau yn fywyd
I deml yr Ysbryd yn nhud fy nhadau.

'Mae amser trwy'r amseroedd
A'i rin gêl yr un ag oedd.
Hen gydymaith pob teithiwr,
Rhydd ei nod ar wedd hen ŵr.
A heddiw hen wyf, ac oeddwn ifanc.
O boen ei ddiwedd nebun ni ddianc.
Tra bwy'n llwch try bun a llanc yn fynych
I fwynaidd edrych ar f'awen ddidranc.

'Eithr o ango huno hun
Credaf, cyfodaf wedyn.
Mae tref a gyfyd i'm trem
Acw, ar seiliau Caersalem.
Awn, seiri hoff, i'w hanian seraffaidd,
E ddaw i'r golwg ein delw ddirgelaidd.
Amser a thrawster ni thraidd i'n hymlid
O glas ieuenctid ei heglwys sanctaidd.

'The good gentle Spirit whispered
His Word to the Virgin Mary.
In His light do you not see
the beauty of Her face?
For her sake I seek the beauty that was revealed
and fine artistry without blemish.
My heart is glad when I find the stones
to be fair and truly firm.

'My sweet Mary, the tender mother long ago,
every one of them is dear.
But the Word which was in Your lap
was beloved above all.
One wish was born to me,
to hold the chisel until death comes,
and hew my days into a life
for the Spirit's temple in the land of my fathers.

'There is a time through all times
whose hidden essence is ever the same.
Old companion of every traveller,
it leaves its mark on an old man's face.
And today I am old, and once I was young.
None can escape from the pain of his end.
When I am dust, maid and lad will often turn
to gaze tenderly on my immortal art.

'Yet I believe that I will rise again
from the oblivion of slumber.
A town rises up before my eyes
yonder, on Jerusalem's foundations.
Let us go, dear craftsmen, to its seraphic essence,
our mysterious image comes into view.
Time and oppression will not penetrate to drive us
from its holy church's sanctuary of youth.

'Uchel fodd a chelfyddyd
Ddi-baid canrifoedd y byd
Islaw, sy'n y ddinas lân,
Crog y fynachlog wychlan,
Urddas y gangell a'i harddwisg yngo
A'r dyfnder tawel i'r sawl a'i gwelo.
Ac yma cyfyd bryd bro Bae San Ffraid
Ond ery enaid ei geinder yno,

'A dawn llon eneidiau'n llu
O'r oesoedd gyda'r Iesu,
Yn ddidlawd eu molawdau
Yn uwch eu hoen o'u hiacháu.
Prydferth arial y parod ferthyri
Yno heb liw hen friw mae Gwenfrewi,
A glanaf, mwynaf i mi o holl ryw
Deheulaw Oen Duw, wele ein Dewi.'

III

Ar gadernid Carn Llidi
Ar hyd un hwyr oedwn i,
Ac yn syn ar derfyn dydd
Gwelwn o ben bwy gilydd
Drwy eitha Dyfed y rhith dihafal,
Ei thresi swnd yn eurwaith ar sindal
Lle naid y lli anwadal yn sydyn
I fwrw ei ewyn dros far a hual.

Gwe arian ar ei goror
Yw mân ynysoedd y môr.
Yno daw canu dyhir
A dawns ton ar ridens tir.
A thanaf y maith ymylwaith melyn,
Fe dry i'r glannau fodrwyog linyn,
Yno gwêl y tonnau gwyn—yn eu llwch
Dan eira'n harddwch o dan Drwyn Hwrddyn.

'The high manner and never-ending
art of all the centuries of the world
below is in the fair city,
the cross of the magnificent monastery,
the chancel's splendour and its finery there
and the quiet depth for those who see it.
And here rises the desire of the land of St Bride's Bay,
but the soul of its beauty remains there,

'and the joyfulness of a host of souls
from all ages with Jesus,
singing rich praises
with vigour renewed by healing,
Lovely vivacity of the willing martyrs.
There without the old wound's stain is Gwenfrewi,
and the fairest, the gentlest of all who sit
at the right hand of the Lamb of God, behold our David.'

III

I lingered one evening
on the stronghold of Carn Llidi,
and with amazement at day's end
I saw from end to end
throughout Dyfed the matchless vision,
its tresses of sand golden on silk
where the inconstant tide suddenly leaps
to cast its foam over bar and bank.

The tiny islands of the sea
are a silver web on its edge.
Long singing comes there
and the waves' dance on the fringes of the land.
And below me the long yellow border,
a curling line turns to the shores,
see there the white waves
with the beauty of powdery snow beneath Hwrddyn's Point.

A rhwysg y diweddar haf
Ar daen trwy'r fro odanaf
A llonyddwch lle naddwyd
Y goron lom, y garn lwyd,
A'm huchelgaer a'i threm uwch y weilgi
A'r gwenyg eilchwyl ar greigiau'n golchi
Rhyw hen dangnefedd fel gweddi ddirgel,
Mae anwes dawel am Ynys Dewi.

A daw ataf o'm deutu
Iaith fwyn hen bethau a fu
Fel caneuon afonydd
Llawer doe dan goed yn gudd.
Aberoedd mân a fu'r beirdd i minnau,
Canent lle rhedent o rwyll y rhydiau,
A thôn yn y pwll ni thau oedd eu naid
A Bae San Ffraid, ebe sŵn y ffrydiau.

Mi chwiliais a dymchwelyd
Mesurau bach amser byd.
Er ymlid, hen Garn Llidi,
O'r oesau taer drosot ti
Anniflan heddiw yw'r hen flynyddoedd
Cans yma mae mynydd fy mynyddoedd
A'i hug o rug fel yr oedd pan glybu'r
Canu ar antur y cynnar wyntoedd.

A doe cynheuodd Dewi
Dan y maen ei dân i mi,
Nes o glos eglwys y glyn
Seiniau ysgafn sy'n esgyn.
Y Fam Wyryol, Ave Maria,
I'r Duw eglured y Deo Gloria,
A chlod a uchel leda y byd
Yn glog ar fywyd o Glegyr Foia.

With the splendour of late summer
spread out in the land below me
and stillness where the bare crown
was hewn, the grey outcrop,
and my high fortresss looking out over the sea
and the waves once more washing over the rocks,
some old peace like a secret prayer,
there is a silent embrace around David's Island.

And there comes to me from all sides
the sweet language of things long ago
like the songs of rivers
in days gone by hidden beneath trees.
The poets were little estuaries to me,
they sang where they flowed from the lattice of the fords,
and their leap was a ceaseless tune in the pool
and St Bride's Bay, said the sound of streams.

I searched and overturned
the little measures of worldly time.
Although the urgent ages have fled
over you, old Carn Llidi,
the old mountains stand firm today
for here is the mountain of my mountains
with its covering of heather as it was when it heard
the early winds sing to and fro.

And yesterday David lit
a fire for me under the stone,
so that sounds rise lightly up
from the refuge of the church in the valley.
The Virgin Mother, Ave Maria,
how clear is the Deo Gloria to God,
and praise spreading high above the world
is a cloak over life from Clegyr Foia.

Egnïon a gyneuodd
Rhwng bwâu yn rhyngu bodd.
Ar rith yr awyr weithion
Clywaf dincial dyfal donc
A chrefftwyr taer uwch yr hoffter terwyn
Yn mynnu ceinder o'r meini cyndyn.
Harddu camp eu gordd a'u cŷn drwy eu hoes
I'r Awen a'u rhoes ar weun y Rhosyn.

Aeddfed fedr i'r Ddyfed fau!
Hirfaith oedd tinc eu harfau,
A chan afiaith cywaith cu
Di-dlawd eu hadeiladu.
Cadarn gynghanedd cydraen ganghennau,
Dwyres odl oesol hyd yr ystlysau,
Gwig, a siffrwd pêr paderau trwyddi—
Rhyw si yn nrysi Rhosyn yr Oesau.

Ond gwych a fu hendai gynt
A sarhad amser ydynt.
A'r mynydd a'i rym anwel
A wysiodd im oes a ddêl,
A distaw ddyfod y cadarn arni,
A saib y treisiwr is y bwtresi.
Chwap, yn y rhestr ffenestri edrychodd
A'r hwb a loriodd y dewr bileri.

A llan a fu dan hen dŵr
Ydyw tud y datodwr.
Mae ei wyrdd yn y murddyn.
Mae'r haul rhwng y muriau hyn
A'i leuer yn ail a'r glaw a'r niwloedd.
Y rhawg yn nhrofa ei hir ganrifoedd
Pan fo blin y drycinoedd, defaid gwâr
A dyr am seintwar o'r stormus wyntoedd.

He set alight energies
between arches bringing satisfaction.
On the illusion of air I hear now
the tinkle of blow upon blow
and fervent craftsmen over the passionate delight
drawing fine art from the stubborn stones.
The achievement of their hammer and chisel all their lives
created beauty of the Spirit which put them on the Rose's moor.

What a mature skill is in my Dyfed!
Long was the sound of their tools,
and with the zest of happy cooperation
they built opulently.
The strong *cynghanedd* of branches in parallel,
twin rows of eternal rhyme along the sides,
a forest, with the whisper of sweet prayers through it—
a murmuring in the thicket of the Rose of the Ages.

But the old houses of long ago were splendid
and they are a rebuke to time
And the mountain with its unseen power
summoned to me an age to come,
and the silent coming of the mighty upon it,
and the ravisher's sojourn beneath the buttresses.
In a flash, he looked through the row of windows
and the blow flattened the brave pillars.

The sanctuary which was once below the old tower
is the territory of the dismantler.
His green is in the ruin.
The sun shines through these walls
and its light alternates with rain and mists.
In the winding of the long centuries to come
when the weather is harsh, tame sheep
will seek shelter from the stormy winds.

Ond ar hyn, myned y rhith.
Gwynnach oedd sofl y gwenith.
Gwelwn ar ôl ei gilio
Hael fron y barhaol fro.
Parabl y nawdd tra pery blynyddoedd
Yw llafur caeau a phreiddiau ffriddoedd.
Daw'r un haul wedi'r niwloedd, a buan
Y daw'r adar cân wedi'r drycinoedd.

A hin glaear cawn glywed
Rhyw loyw anturio ar led,
A'i wyrdd reng drwy bridd yr âr
Yw'r ceirch yn torri carchar.
A llawer heuwr hirgam fu'n amau
Mai mwy ei dynged na chwmwd angau,
A heuodd rhwng ei gloddiau dangnefedd
A rhodio'i dudwedd i'r oed â'i dadau.

Hŷn na'i dŷ awen Dewi
A hwy ei saernïaeth hi.
A darn trech na dyrnod drom
Yr angau, ei air rhyngom,
A rhuddin Crist trwy ganghennau Cristion
Er siantau taer teulu'r seintiau tirion
Gwylia o hyd yn y galon gywir
A byth adwaenir yn obaith dynion.

Y ffordd, y bywyd ni phaid,
Y gwirionedd gâr enaid
A phren y rhagorol ffrwyth,
A'r Hwsmon a'r iau esmwyth.
Ac yn y galon mae Ei hwsmonaeth
Ac Yntau'n aros ar gant ein hiraeth,
Digon i gymydogaeth a digon
I ieuo'r hilion trwy'r ddaear helaeth.

But at this, the illusion disappeared.
The wheat stubble was whiter.
After it fled I saw
this lasting countryside's bountiful breast.
The crops of the fields and the meadows' flocks
speak of security whilst the years continue.
The same sun comes after the mists,
and the birds' song quickly returns after the storms.

In mild weather we can hear
a bright adventuring abroad,
and its green rank through the arable soil
are the oats breaking out of prison.
And many a long-pacing sower has felt
that his fate is greater than death's commote,
and he sowed peace between his hedges
and walked his land to meet his fathers.

David's spirit is older than his house
and its design is greater.
Mightier than death's heavy blow
is his word amongst us,
and Christ's strength through the branches of the Christian,
for the fervent chants of the family of gentle saints,
watches still in the true heart
and will always be known as the hope of mankind.

The way, the life will not cease,
the truth which the soul loves
and the tree of finest fruit,
the Husbandman with the easy yoke.
His husbandry is in the heart
and He waits on the rim of our yearning,
enough for a community and enough
to yoke together the races throughout the wide world.

Ac ar y llain ger y lli
Y rhoed iau ar war Dewi,
Rhychor y Duw Goruchel
A thir serth ni thyr ei sêl.
Y ddaear lawn hon sy'n ddarlun heno,
Twysennau grawn yn y teisi'n gryno,
Pob cynhaeaf mi gaf gofio Geilwad
Hen rym ei dyniad a'r iau amdano.

Nos da, gymwynas Dewi,
A'i dir nawdd. Dyro i ni,
Yr un wedd, yr hen addaw
A thŷ llwyth nid o waith llaw.
Trwy'r grug lliw gwin troi o'r graig lle gweinwyd
I mi'r heddwch a ddaliai fy mreuddwyd,
A rhiniol oes y garn lwyd oedd gennyf,
A'i gwên, a chennyf y gân ni chanwyd.

And on the strip of land by the sea
a yoke was put on David's shoulders,
the ploughing ox of Almighty God
whose zeal is not broken by steep land.
This full earth is an image tonight,
ears of corn gathered into stacks,
at every harvest I call to mind an Ox-driver,
the old strength of his pulling with the yoke about him.

Goodnight, David's favour
and his sanctuary. Give to us,
in the same way, the old promise
and a house for the tribe not made by man's hand.
Through the wine-coloured heather from the rock where you served
send me the peace which held my dream,
and the good age of grey rock which I once possessed,
and its smile, and in my head the song which has not been sung.

NOTES TO THE POEMS

Cwm Berllan, p. 64. Cwm Berllan, that is, Orchard Valley.

Daw'r Wennol yn ôl i'w nyth (The Swallow will find her nest) p.78.
The War Office took over this district in 1939. But some Preseli sheep winter there. (W.W.)

Diwedd Bro (The end of a Countryside) p. 82.
In the Third Branch of the *Mabinogion*, Pryderi, lord of the seven cantrefs of Dyfed, took Manawydan with Rhiannon and Cigfa their wives to feast in Arberth. After a crack of thunder came a mist so thick they could not see one another; and when that lifted they found that all seven cantrefs were deserted, all the people and animals stolen away by a spell. For a year they lived alone. Then Manawydan said to Pryderi, 'We cannot live like this. Let us make for Lloegr (England) and learn some craft to earn our livelihood.' And they made for England.

Llŷr was Manawydan's father, and originally a sea-god. The poem also refers to the legend of Cantre'r Gwaelod, the 'one' cantref of the first line, a fair land now under the tide because of a drunken watchman not keeping the seawalls safe.

Brawdoliaeth (Brotherhood) p. 88.
Written in 1940 for Gwynfor Evans, later the president of Plaid Cymru, who asked him to contribute to a series of pacifist pamphlets.

Ar Weun Cas' Mael (On Weun Cas' Mael) p. 94.
When Waldo lived at Cas-mael (Puncheston) he was fairly close to the large armaments depot at Trecŵn. A 'waun' or 'weun' is a marsh or moorland.

Adnabod (Acknowledge) p. 108.
The title offers particular problems to the translator.
Adnabod is a verb-noun with a much wider meaning than any comparable word in English. It means primarily 'to know a person'—French *connaître*, as opposed to *savoir*, 'to know a thing'—but it also means 'to acknowledge' or 'to be acquainted with' or 'to recognise kinship with'; and it can mean 'to have carnal knowledge of'. At the cost of some awkwardness I have kept the verbal form as a name, and selected the meaning for opportunist reasons: 'Acknowledge' rhymes with knowledge. *Adnabod* is a keyword in Waldo's

208

poetry, but usually it is possible to find a suitable paraphrase for it. Here it is not: either you accept one or other awkwardness, or you don't translate the poem at all.

Caniad Ehedydd (Lark Song) p. 114.

Branwen, isolated and abused in Ireland by her husband the king, sent a message by means of her pet starling to her brother Brân, who came from Wales to rescue her.

Cymru'n Un (Wales One) p. 120.

Hiraethog in west Denbighshire, famous in literary tradition as the home of several writers, was the area where his mother's family came from. His father's family came from rural east Pembrokeshire, where many of the people migrated 'over Mynydd Du' into the coal-mining valleys of Glamorgan. Waldo was thus a product of both north and south Wales—'In me is Wales one.' His own homeland was, of course, the district round the Preseli hills in Pembrokeshire.

Mewn Dau Gae (In Two Fields) p. 132.

Weun Parc y Blawd and Parc y Blawd—two fields in Pembrokeshire.

End of verse 5: *Revelation* 22, 2. 'And the leaves of the tree were for the healing of the nations.' (W.W.)

Geneth Ifanc (A Young Girl) p. 140.

In Avebury Museum, from an early village on nearby Windmill Hill. About 2500 B.C. (W.W.)

Angharad p. 144.

Angharad, wife of Ieuan Llwyd of Glyn Aeron, had the gown of scarlet in Dafydd ap Gwilym's elegy for her. The Angharad here was my mother. (W.W.)

Gyfaill, mi'th gofiaf (I remember a friend) p. 146.

Idwal Jones (1895-1937), playwright and humourist, college friend and collaborator with Waldo in many parodies and satires.

Tri Bardd o Sais a Lloegr (Three English Poets and England) p. 148.

I. Thomas Hardy. See the beginning of *The Dynasts*.

II. John Keats. Winchester was a centre of cultivation for the Belgae before the Romans came. The poet stayed here in September 1819, a visit very productive for his poetry, 'the leaves of his tree,' as he called it; 'This world is a vale of soul making' is from a letter.

III. William Cowper. 'I was a stricken deer and left the herd.' And when his country was rejoicing in the victories of the Seven Years War, 'O for a lodge in some vast wilderness.' (W.W.)

Waldo visited England with Linda in the Spring of 1940, at the height of his depression about the outbreak of war. They went to the Quantocks, where Wordsworth and Coleridge wrote *The Lyrical Ballads*. After Linda's death in 1943, he left Wales to teach in several places in England. This poem combines memories from both these times.

Yn Nyddiau'r Cesar (In the Days of Caesar) p. 158.

The epigraph is mine (T.C.): the original refers in the first line to the 'counting of subjects' for taxation purposes.

'But thou, Bethlehem Ephratah, though thou be little among the thousands of Judah, yet out of thee shall come forth unto me that is to be ruler; whose goings forth have been from of old, from everlasting.' *Micah*, V, 2

'How think ye? If a man have an hundred sheep, and one of them be gone astray, doth he not leave the ninety and nine, and goeth into the mountains, and seeketh that which is gone astray?' *Matthew*, XVIII, 12

God is conceived as a 'pencerdd' a chief poet of heaven, composing his *awdl*, a metrical tour-de-force with full *cynghanedd*, the strict yet flexible mixture of cross-alliteration and rhyme that is unique to Welsh bardic poetry. Literally the last line would be: 'The chief poet of heaven is searching us as words for his *awdl*.'

Eneidfawr (Great-Soul) p. 160.

This poem was written on the way home to Lyneham after I'd been with the London Indians at the Gandhi memorial service. (W.W.)

The title imitates the names in Bunyan.

Gwenallt p. 174.

'There is at Jerusalem by the sheep market a pool, which is called in the Hebrew tongue Bethesda, having five porches. In these lay a great multitude of impotent folk, of blind, halt, withered, waiting for the movement of the water. For an angel went down at a certain season into the pool, and troubled the water; whosoever then first after the troubling of the water stepped in was made whole of whatsoever disease he had.' *John*, 5, 2-4

It was where Jesus said to the lame man, 'Rise, take up thy bed, and walk.' Gwenallt was a great poet, Christian and nationalist, and physically a small man with very wrinkled features.

Llandysillio-yn-Nyfed p.178.

Waldo for much of his boyhood lived in or near Llandysilio-yn-Nyfed—that is, St Tysilio's-in-Dyfed—where his father was the headmaster of the primary school. It seems fitting that this, his last poem, should be about the saint of the place that meant so much to him. Tysilio was a lord of Powys in the sixth century who chose the monastic life. He lived in Meifod in Maldwyn—the old Montgomeryshire, proverbial for its gentleness—but had to escape because some of his family tried to make him a prince. There are churches dedicated to him in Pembrokeshire, Carmarthenshire and Anglesey, as well as in Powys.

NOTES TO THE APPENDIX
(T.C.)

Tŷ Dewi (St David's) p. 182.

Most of the place-names in the poem refer to the area round St David's Head (Penmaen Dewi), the northernmost promontory of the Pembrokeshire peninsula, two or three miles north-west of St. David's Cathedral.

Part I

St. 1 Ynys Dewi (here translated as David's Island, but in English usually called Ramsey)—an island S.W. of Penmaen Dewi.

Pen y Fan—according to James Nicholas in conversation, Waldo confessed to him that this was a slip of memory on his part, and it should really have been Pen y Maen, i.e. Penmaen Dewi, St David's head.

Porth Maelgan (or Melgan)—a bay on the south side of Penmaen Dewi.

St. 4 Hwrddyn (Trwynhwrddyn)—a rocky promontory on the S. of Penmaen Dewi.

St. 8 Mynyw or Menevia—the diocese of St David's.

St. 10 Melita's fire—a reference to *Acts* 28, 1-2. When St Paul and his fellow-prisoners were shipwrecked on Malta (called Melita at that time) the inhabitants showed them great kindness, lighting a large fire on the beach for them. Hence, 'Melita's fire' is a kenning or metaphor for the welcome given to the gospel and the saints.

St. 11 Samson—a Celtic saint, originally a monk at Llanilltud Fawr, then abbot of Caldey; but most renowned as one of the founders of the Church in Brittany, where his monastery at Dol was famous. His life is better documented (i.e. earlier and less purely hagiological) than that of most saints of the time. (See *Saints, Seaways and Settlements in the Celtic Lands*, E.G. Bowen, pp. 167-170).

St. 12 Clomen Wen—literally 'White Dove'—St Columba, the Irish founder of the monastery of Iona in the Hebrides from which Scotland was evangelised.

212

St. 14-15 The Birds of Rhiannon and Brân Fendigaid or Bendigeidfran (Brân the Blessed)—Rhiannon ('Great Queen') and Brân were both originally deities. The poem refers to the Second Branch of the *Mabinogion* where, after an unsuccessful invasion of Ireland to rescue his sister, Brân was mortally wounded. His head accompanied the survivors to Otherworld feasts at Harlech and Gwales in Dyfed, carousing with them as though it was still alive. In Harlech, Rhiannon's birds sang to them—'all the singing they'd ever heard was nothing compared to this.'

Part II

St. 3 Dowrog—Dowrog Common, a marshy plain about two miles N.E. of the Cathedral.

St. 4 Your two journeys—Pope Calixtus II (1119-24) officially recognised David as a Saint of the Universal Church in 1120 and gave his cult a great boost by laying it down that two pilgrimages to St David's were equal in merit to one pilgrimage to Rome.

St. 5 Newgwl is today Niwgwl or Newgale—seven miles east of St. David's.

Pedr or Peter the Norman, and Rhys—Peter de Leia was Bishop of Menevia (St David's) at the time when Rhys ap Gruffydd (the Lord Rhys— 1132-97) re-established Deheubarth as a power in Wales. Peter de Leia was responsible for starting the construction of the preŝent Cathedral.

The Rose—St David's was built below and out of sight of the surrounding plateau in the lower part of the valley of the Alun, now called Merry Vale, but then Vallis Rosina or Glyn Rhosyn, usually translated as Vale of Roses; but according to Bowen (op. cit. p, 218) 'Rhosyn' actually derives from 'Rhos' and means 'a small swamp.' 'Rose' however is rich in metaphorical and spiritual significance—we could compare the Biblical *Song of Songs*, 'I am the rose of Sharon and the lily of the Valley,' and the mediaeval 'Rhosyn yr Oesau', 'Rose of the Ages', later in the poem (Part III, st. 8).

St. 14 Bae San Ffraid—St Bride's Bay—the bay between St David's Head in the north of Pembrokeshire and Skomer Island in the south.

St. 15. Gwenfrewi—St Winefred was restored to life by St Beuno after her head had been cut off. Her shrine was at Holywell in Clwyd, where the healing miracles associated with her well still attract many pilgrims.

Part III

St. 1 Carn Llidi—the highest part of Penmaen Dewi, St David's Head.

St. 6 Clegyr Foia or Boia, a settlement about a mile W. of the Cathedral. St David is said to have founded his cell in Glyn Rhosyn (where the Cathedral now stands) after defeating an Irish chieftain named Boia.

St. 8 Cynghanedd—the elaborate system of rhyme and cross-alliteration which bind together the two halves of a line in the Welsh strict metres.